George Armatage

The horseowner and stableman's companion

Hints on the selection, purchase and general management of the horse

George Armatage

The horseowner and stableman's companion
Hints on the selection, purchase and general management of the horse

ISBN/EAN: 9783742833662

Manufactured in Europe, USA, Canada, Australia, Japa

Cover: Foto ©Lupo / pixelio.de

Manufactured and distributed by brebook publishing software (www.brebook.com)

George Armatage

The horseowner and stableman's companion

PORTRAIT OF EMPRESS AND HER FOAL.

THE

HORSEOWNER AND STABLEMAN'S

COMPANION:

OR,

HINTS ON THE SELECTION, PURCHASE, AND GENERAL
MANAGEMENT OF THE HORSE.

BY

GEORGE ARMATAGE, M.R.C.V.S.

EDITOR OF "CLATER'S EVERY MAN HIS OWN CATTLE DOCTOR."

LONDON:
FREDERICK WARNE AND CO.
BEDFORD STREET, COVENT GARDEN.
NEW YORK: SCRIBNER, WELFORD AND CO.

LONDON:
SAVILL, EDWARDS AND CO., PRINTERS, CHANDOS STREET,
COVENT GARDEN.

CONTENTS.

	PAGE
PREFACE	ix

PART I.

MISMANAGEMENT 1

DEVELOPMENT AND MAINTENANCE:

    Immediate Object of Food—Development—Maintenance—Waste or Decay—Importance of Good Food for Young Animals—Evils of an Insufficiency 8

ORGANS OF DIGESTION:

    Enumeration—Prehension—Incisor Teeth—Tongue—Cheeks—Molars or Grinders—Pharynx—Gullet—Deglutition 14

INSALIVATION:

    Saliva — Salivary Glands — Solvent Action — Chemical Action—Quantity of Saliva—Uses and Importance of Saliva 16

STOMACH:

    Peculiarities in the Horse, Ox, and Man—Broken Wind, and Chronic Cough—Rapid Digestion in the Horse — Small Stomach — Necessity for Regular Feeding 20

	PAGE
INTESTINES:	
Enumeration and Division—Length—Small Intestines—Digestion in—Secretions—Chyle—Lacteals—Absorption and Assimilation—Capacity—Large Intestines—Division—Absorption—Capacity	23
THE DIGESTIVE PROCESS:	
A Complex Action—Gastric Digestion—Gastric Juice—Intestinal Digestion—Chyle—Formation of Blood	26
ELEMENTARY PRINCIPLES OF FOOD:	
Enumeration—Flesh Formers—Heat Producers—Salts—Acids—Fœces or Dung	28
ESSENTIAL CHARACTERS OF FOOD:	
Nutritious Principles—Their Identity from all Sources—Non-nutritious Principles—Animal Heat—Necessity for Substances of a Mixed Character—Bulk or Volume	29
ERRORS TO BE AVOIDED:	
Fluids—Cooked Food—Injurious effect of Common Salt—Diabetes and Albuminuria—Farcy and Glanders	40
ADVANTAGES OF PROPER FOOD AND SYSTEM	46
REGULAR FEEDING	50
CALCULI OR STONES:	
Their Origin—Different Kinds—Frequently Prove Fatal	51
OBJECTIONS TO THE USE OF DRY FOOD:	
Do Oats Pass Out Unchanged?—Proofs—Necessity for Healthy Condition—Care Required in Feeding—Importance of a Superintendent	54

Contents.

PART II.

VARIETIES OF FOOD:

 Nutrition in Each — Maize — Oats — Cost of Feeding Upon — Measure and Weight should be Combined 63

SELECTION AND PURCHASE OF GRAIN 68

ECONOMY OF FOOD:

 Indian Corn Injurious — Linseed — Tares — Mixtures Necessary 70

SYSTEMS ADOPTED ON VARIOUS COLLIERY ESTATES:

 Hunting on Cut Food — Hetton System 74

WHAT CONSTITUTES A CHEAP FOOD 81

OBJECTIONS TO A CHANGE OF GRAIN 82

BRAN, ITS NATURE, USES, AND ABUSES 83

LONDONDERRY COLLIERY SYSTEM:

 Mixture — Steamed Food — Waste, &c. 85

FORMS OF ADMIXTURE:

 Low Rates — High Rates 89

GREEN FOOD, ITS BENEFIT AND INJURY 97

ECONOMY IN USING CHAFF AND BRUISED CORN . 99

PEA AND BEAN STRAW 101

SAVING TO BE EFFECTED 102

IMPORTANCE OF GROOMING 104

PART III.

SELECTION AND PURCHASE OF HORSES:

    Tricks and Frauds of Dealers—Bribery—Warranty—Certificates of Soundness—Recommending Horses—Precautions to be observed 111

STABLE MANAGEMENT:

    Early Operations in the Stable—Watering—Purity of Water—Cleanliness—Disinfectants—Lighting of Stables—Ventilation—Various Plans—Heat or Temperature of the Stable—Grooming or Dressing—Stable Tools—Washing the Legs—Bandages—Clothing—Bedding—Disposal of Manure—Clipping and Singeing 128

FEEDING:

    Oats—Beans—Barley—Tares or Lentils—Hay—Straw—Bran—Linseed—Linseed or Oil-cake—Maize or Indian Corn—Locust or Carob Bean—Condiments—Vegetable Food—Turning to Grass—Regularity of Feeding—Feeding after Work 156

EXERCISE 181

CONDITION 185

THE TURKISH OR ROMAN BATH, AND WASHING HORSES AFTER HUNTING 189

GENERAL ARRANGEMENT OF STABLES:

    Ordinary Arrangement Defective—Improvement on the Plan—Paving of Stable Floors—Drains—Declivity of Stable Floors—Wooden Floors—Their Economy—Loose Boxes 194

Contents.

PAGE

THE CAUSES OF DISEASE, AND ITS PREVENTION:
  Prevention Better than Cure 203

SIMPLE RULES FOR SHOEING, AND MANAGEMENT OF
    THE FEET OF HORSES:
  The Hoof—Wall—Sole and Frog—Nails—Shoes—
    Their Shape—Bar Shoes—Leather Soles—Stopping
    for Feet—Foot Ointments—Cutting and Brushing
    —Groggy Feet—Sidebones—Pumiced Feet—Pricks
    and Binds—Shoeing in Coal Mines 208

POULTICES AND FOMENTATIONS 222

SENDING FOR THE VETERINARY SURGEON 224

PREFACE.

It has been said, "What England is, she has been made by the thinking and working of many generations," and the remark has an application quite as special to the British stockowner as to the merchant prince.

By the concentration of talent and English perseverance the stock of Great Britain has been raised to a standard of unparalleled excellence. Throughout the operations of agriculture have kept this end prominently in view, and with unparalleled excellence has been also derived a proportionate collateral value. Both are qualities which call for regard, and forcibly point out the necessity for an orthodox system of preservation. But neither—successful as they have become—are the result of outside assistance, which, as in other countries, the agriculturist and horseowner can obtain on the most approved and easy principles. They are due to the patient working and deep intelligence which forms one of the innate portions of English character.

Preface.

All the advice and assistance which veterinary science has almost up to the present time furnished to the stockowner in the works to which he has had access, have been far below the requirements of the age, and shrouded beneath faulty detail and even positive error, the result of young and recent observation. Much inconvenience, mischief, and vexation has been caused by exclusive attention to *effects*, while the *causes* have been altogether overlooked. The greater part of the mortality among live stock is *preventible*, and, to demonstrate that, it is required that the causes of disease should be clearly understood. A scientific estimate of the animal body, its habits, and nature has led to that understanding, and the irrefragable proof; and both will become more apparent day by day, as scientific truths are submitted to the thinking and working community. By these means we are daily adding fresh stores of information in that department which relates to the preservation of animal life; and one of the great principles is to obtain a thorough acquaintance with the laws of health which always rightly precedes a study of the laws of disease. Horsekeepers, stockfeeders, and flockmasters require the first in order to adopt a correct system of prevention, rather than seek disappointment in practising curative measures, the true nature and variations of which they can have neither the time nor the opportunity to understand properly.

These truths have prompted the author to treat rather fully the subject of the physiology of digestion—nature of food—principles by which economy and safety to animal life may be gained, as well as other equally important matters which come within the notice of all who have horses under their care. With a correct knowledge of the healthy functions of animal life must ensue greater respect for the fabric which has been termed "the tuneful harp of a thousand strings," and a correspondingly increased desire and ability to put into force the valuable precepts which are acquired by the lesson. The preservation of our domestic animals is a comprehensive subject, and has been eminently fruitful in many places already where it has met with even an ordinary consideration. It is the desire of the author to direct his efforts towards increasing the success of the movement, and he feels assured the present volume will prove no slight aid where the disposition to improve exists. The non-professional reader has been considered throughout. Technicalities have been suppressed as far as practicable, or supplemented by explanatory addenda, which it is hoped will bring the work directly into the hands of all who have animals placed under their care; and succeed in the diffusion of useful knowledge in a direction where tradition has so long and uselessly held a seat, to the immense sacrifice of one of the greatest sources of national wealth—our domestic animals.

 Eastlake Road,
  Camberwell, S.E.

THE
HORSEOWNER AND STABLEMAN'S COMPANION.

PART I.

MISMANAGEMENT.

MISMANAGEMENT in any department is universally acknowledged to be the precursor of evil consequences, and one of the golden rules in our social economy is that which teaches how to recognise the one and avert the other.

If there is a section of the community which languidly basks in the oblivion of misrule more than another, it is that under whose care are placed our valuable domestic animals, and to which we trace deterioration of breed, prevalence of disease, and a high rate of mortality.

As things at present exist in the many places to which these remarks apply, one would be inclined to the opinion that the study of *system* in the stable and cow-shed is unworthy the time, trouble, attention, or altogether useless: hence the result; valuable animals are left to the care of illiterate attendants, who prescribe for their wants and comforts under predominate ignorance. At one time they are fed with extravagance, and at another a nutritious meal is denied them.

Unwarranted officiousness also too frequently provides a novel system, and wonders are speedily developed in adverse of a desirable state, while indisputable obstinacy and prejudice prevent the recognition of cause and effect.

In ignorance of the nature of food, principles of feeding and management, the annual losses from indigestion and its consequences among horses and cattle are somewhat startling, and unfortunately too common throughout Great Britain. Even in places where we have a right to expect practical information on the laws of health and the animal economy, confusion only remains. This is particularly the case upon some of the large colliery establishments in the north of England.

Immense numbers of horses and ponies are here fed in accordance with principles laid down by a "land agent," upon corn usually purchased by himself. These principles are generally original, and resemble the laws of the "Medes and Persians" in being unalterable.

During one part of the year, corn with an excess of green food is supplied; at another, the grain is spoiled by steaming; each period being regulated in total ignorance and disregard of existing conditions, *without instituting the least inquiry in most cases, and never making a descent of the mines* to examine the animals which come in for a share of such magnanimous solicitude.

Besides this functionary, there are other members of the executive called "viewers," who do not forget their exalted position, attained in some instances, I fear, at a speed which has not admitted of the mind assuming an adaptability to it; at least, judging from the amount of presumption with which these men vaunt their opinions upon professional matters, and in their want of respect to others infinitely higher in the social scale.

Under such principles of "graudeeism," it is not surprising that, with unsystematic feeding, hard work unnecessarily protracted, with cruelty overlooked or connived at, mortality is excessive. The ears of reason are, however, stopped, and as some one must bear blame when it is forthcoming, he who possesses the least influence in the matter —the resident veterinary surgeon—receives the whole in a most ignominious manner.

Happily all are not of this kind.

Some of my best friends are engaged in the management of extensive collieries, and have amply shown what can be done to ameliorate the life and condition of the poor creatures employed there. Such bear a remarkable contrast to the former class, who never recognise the efforts of others except when they can be appropriated as their own good deeds, by which they seek the adulation of the owner, and swamp into insignificance him who feels it an imperative duty to utter a word for reform or economy. This is the "red-tape," for the exercise of which I presume owners who know it not pay rather dearly.

It has been known that reports detailing the existence of glaring evils easily remedied by a change of system, requiring no extra outlay, but insuring a highly profitable investment, drawn up by able men — veterinary surgeons — who have studied these matters for years and practised them successfully, and who, after sending them to headquarters by desire, have been treated contemptuously—such men have been told, "*your information is only a parcel of figures,*" or after being summoned to the office of the "viewer," "*you had better not interfere in such matters; things have gone along very well hitherto, and no complaint has been made from above; you receive your salary, and it will be advisable that you should not report these things beyond myself.*"

Existing affairs are permitted to go on as before, but the information thus obtained is put aside, in order to be applied as perfectly original matter at a time when the proper owner is not present to identify it.

A few years ago, in a paper read before a certain farmers' club, I gave the details of a system of feeding colliery horses which had been successfully carried on by the resident veterinary surgeon some years, and resulted in the annual saving of hundreds of pounds.

The local newspapers gave full reports, the

executive was jealous of the honour given, and immediately took the feeding into their own hands.

On another occasion Mr. Hunting, M.R.C.V.S., attended the Newcastle Farmers' Club, in obedience to a request, to detail the system which he had carried out successfully both as to the saving of expenditure and preventing mortality. The usual feeling of malice and jealousy prevailed here also, for some unknown person forwarded a parcel of hay-seeds and rubbish to the chairman, with the statement that the sample was taken from the kind of provender which Mr. Hunting used, and was about to recommend to the meeting.

Such is the treatment with which professional men are met upon some of the extensive colliery estates of Britain. Instructions received from "head-quarters" point out the necessity for surveillance over the provender, mode of feeding, work, &c., by the veterinary-surgeon; but to detect an error and point it out as required, although an enormous saving would accrue from a change, is to render him odious in the eyes of despotism. If he wishes to hold his appointment, it must be by the sacrifice of conscientious duty, an assumed blindness to, and perfect silence upon, such topics. If he persists in his course, the results are known only to himself.

While this treatment is permitted, it is not very likely that great improvements, or the avoidance of unnecessary expenditure, waste, and mortality will take place in the departments referred to. Owners may still complain about the disparity between profits and expenses. Efficient veterinary surgeons (and there are men in the body of practitioners as valuable in their calling as viewers are in theirs), desirous of establishing necessary and profitable reformation in departments *essentially their own*, lose interest, and weary in well-doing after repeated insults of the kind referred to are heaped upon them. They are not allowed a word in explanation, and at length retire in disgust, and the places are filled by automatons—mere machines—who generally occupy such posts with greater satisfaction to those who fill up the executive and revel in the exercise of despotic power.

It is not only in reference to colliery animals where mismanagement occurs. We need but turn our attention to the system pursued in our large town and farm stables; and cattle and sheep also are found to participate in the general results.

Veterinary surgeons in some districts can testify to the bulk of their cases being those which arise from indigestion, and the insurance papers of many a defunct society would afford doleful tales of sudden death from the same states, causing rupture of the stomach, intestines, or diaphragm, calculi (or stones), and incurable diabetes running into farcy and glanders.

Farmers are fully conversant with similar results also, which find an origin in the cheap and inferior bean or pea straw, musty hay, and supposed economical system of feeding with little or no corn.

Among his cattle he endures losses from engorged and ruptured stomach, splenic apoplexy, black-leg, parturient diseases, diarrhœa, and dysentery; and among his sheep, in addition to the above, skin and parasitic diseases.

The London brewers have to lament the loss of their plump dray horses from rupture and disease of the liver; and Scotch proprietors suffer no less, though rather differently, from the use of trashy boiled mixtures of food.

In the coal mines, where proper surveillance is not permitted, and stupid customs are adhered to, indigestion, with its attendant states, carries off many valuable lives, and the cause is looked upon as inducing a condition which must be endured, or the evil as a manifestation of some peculiar influence, probably of a planetary character.

Notwithstanding this, all busy themselves in searching for a *cure*, without going further to attempt a solution of the mystery, which may be interpreted by the principle of *prevention*. We thus go on in blindness and obstinacy, seeking after some brilliant theory, and in eager pursuit of that which is remote, neglect the highly profitable and easily deciphered lessons which, already pregnant with most ample information, are completely within the grasp.

DEVELOPMENT AND MAINTENANCE.

A discussion of the subject of food and its application to the animal fabric, involves a consideration of scientific principles which reveal the exact nature of the substances employed, their transformation within the organism, and the offices they perform at their destination.

The *immediate object of food* is the development and maintenance of the animal body.

Development may be briefly stated to be that process by which the various parts or organs assume their relative form, size, and capabilities for functional activity—*e.g.*, secretion, excretion, and the like. Development is principally referable to intra-uterine life, or that period during which the future animal lies within the womb of its mother, when the various organs, as the brain, heart, lungs, liver, and in fact all parts of the body, are acquiring their peculiar and characteristic form.

Each primitive portion gradually and constantly receives fresh additions, and each stage constitutes also a farther elaboration and assumption of higher powers.

Development continues also throughout a period after birth. The long-legged, weedy-looking foal is an example excellently suitable for the purpose of illustration. Although as far as internal organs are concerned, development may be said to be in a measure complete, yet there are important changes to be otherwise effected. The muscles of the body are small and pale, and the bones (so called) are very deficient in osseous material (earthy salts). A few teeth only are through the gums, and others are lying in different stages beneath in the form of a highly vascular pulp, quite unlike its future self.

In each there are important changes to take place.

The bundles of cartilage in the centre of the limbs and beneath the muscles of the body, &c., gradually become harder, and lose their characteristic elasticity. Their structure is altered by the deposition of bony material, and by and bye we have the osseous framework or skeleton completed.

The pale muscular fibres assume greater dimensions, and at the same time a darker colour, and power to act more forcibly on the individual bones.

The tooth pulp within the gums, already provided with innumerable blood vessels and nerves, gradually acquires the shape of a tooth, incisor or molar, its different layers of hard substance variously termed dentine, enamel, &c., and only at a specified time will it appear above the surface.

At length the animal is "filled up," "made up," or "furnished," in stable phraseology, and the period of *youth* gives way to that which is known as the *adult stage*.

Maintenance has been going on throughout the whole of this time. Functional activity is attended by a process of *waste* or *decay* of the parts implicated. This process will be hereafter expressed as *metamorphosis of tissues*.

In no period of life can this process be said to be dormant or non-existent, but in none so slow or so little required as in early youth. At this time the building up of the animal body by the accumulation of blood, bone, muscle, hoof, horn, teeth, hair, &c., &c., is actively carried on, and their waste or decay comparatively small. In adult life, however, when development has gone on to completion, and great exertion is called forth, metamorphosis or change in the constitution of the tissues above mentioned is great.

This requires the process of maintenance or repair to restore, during repose, that which has being constantly lost during activity or exercise.

The movements of the arms or legs in walking, the tongue and jaws in speaking, lungs during respiration, heart in its beating, and intestines during contraction,—in short, any act, voluntary or involuntary, which calls forth muscular movements in any part of the animal body, is attended with the expenditure of vital force, as shown in the change or alteration of the condition, waste, decay, or metamorphosis of the composing material.

During metamorphosis of tissue chemical

Development and Maintenance. 11

action is instituted, and new compounds are produced which are no longer useful to the body. They are called *effete* materials, and after being collected by appropriate vessels termed *lymphatics*, are by them conveyed to special organs for the purpose of being expelled. If retained, they would prove highly detrimental to the body, and even destructive to life.

The *waste of muscular tissue* from work and ordinary exercise is considerable, that substance forming a great portion of the animal body. It is constantly in need of fresh material to restore or replace those parts which have been removed by waste, and the elements necessary are provided by the food, after undergoing important changes hereafter to be mentioned under digestion.

Such facts, briefly as they are detailed, and divested, as far as practicable, of technicalities, present most important points to view, and enable us to direct particular attention to the application and economising of material (food) for the production of the greatest amount of actual force—strength and vigour in working animals, or of fat in those destined for the butcher.

With these before us, the effects of some of the modes in which animals are kept, will be clearly understood.

Under the subject of development it has been stated the process is confined to intra-uterine life and early periods of youth. It is then we find the great demands upon the system in order to complete the formation and building up of the whole body. Every one almost knows that much more food than ordinarily is consumed by the pregnant mare or cow, and that the young animal consumes much food of a nutritious quality without the appearance being in all cases obviously benefited thereby.

These illustrations serve to show the great demands for blood, bone, muscle, skin, hair, hoof, tendons, &c. &c., and a moment's reflection will cause one to pause and wonder how some persons can really expect to make a horse, cow, or other animal upon the quantities of miserable rubbish which are put in the poor creatures' way when young.

How they can witness their colts and calves standing without cover in an empty straw-yard or bare pasture in the cold and rain during the winter, and expect the grass of the coming summer will make up for the previous starvation, is indeed a paradox. It appears quite sufficient with some that a horse should taste corn only when he is able to earn it, and cattle when they commence to give milk, or there are prospects of their being useful to the butcher.

All this is mistaken policy. The young horse or ox requires ample food for the building up of the frame, and we discern the wise provision of nature in furnishing the rich elements in the milk of the mother. Both need highly nutritious food, and when this is denied, the owner finds he is on the sure road towards spoiling them. They always suffer acutely when good food is afterwards given; the change serves only to engender serious, if not fatal, disease. Instances will be found in the maladies *black-leg* or *quarter-evil*, *splenic apoplexy*, *blain*, &c., of cattle and sheep.

In the horse we find, when put to work for the first time, he is "unable to stand the corn;" the legs swell, coat stares, he performs his work badly, and there are other indications of a disordered state within.

Colic, or *purpura hæmorrhagica*, speedily kills him, or he is left to dole out a miserable existence with protracted suffering from *chronic disease of the lungs* or *liver, diabetes, canker, laminitis* (founder), constant attacks of *lymphangitis* (weed), and *farcy*, terminating, after effectually propagating the contagion, in *glanders* and *death*.

As life and development proceeds, food then serves a different purpose. While it is expended in supplying fresh elements to the blood, that fluid has now to furnish elaborate materials to replace the constituents of the body lost during waste of muscle and other tissues, which are rendered visible in the shape of the products of respiration, perspiration, the urine, and fæces. What formerly went to form muscle, bone, &c., now goes to repair them. The blood in all cases is the fluid which furnishes the *pabulum* whence tissues derive their support. That fluid is maintained by regular additions of elements obtained from the food. The process which prepares them we have to consider shortly.

ORGANS OF DIGESTION.

The organs of digestion comprise the *mouth, teeth, tongue, salivary glands, pharynx, œsophagus* or *gullet, stomach, intestines, liver,* and *pancreas* or *sweetbread.*

In connexion with the mouth we find appropriate muscles forming the bulk of the lips and sides for the *prehension* or gathering of food, and *incisor teeth* or *nippers*—six above and below in the horse, and eight only below in the ox, sheep, deer, &c.—for the purpose of cutting off the herbage. Within the mouth the *tongue* performs the important office of distinguishing by the peculiar sense of taste, the difference in each variety of substances introduced, and moves them from side to side in order to bring them within the pressure of the *molar teeth* or *grinders*. The *tongue* at length, by a contraction upon itself backwards, carries the bolus of food with it, which is then seized by the pharynx, and passes immediately along the gullet to the stomach.

The *cheeks* on each side being formed of

Organs of Digestion. 15

muscles, assist materially in keeping the food effectually between the molar teeth. Through their substance pass ducts or tubes which convey necessary lubricating and solvent fluids to the mouth.

The *molars* or *grinders* are twenty-four in number, six of which are situated above and below upon each side of the jaws in the back part of the mouth. In order to observe them particularly the mouth must be held wide open.

They are large and rough upon the wearing surface, and form most perfect agents in crushing and grinding, or masticating the hard grain and kernels which this animal requires as natural food.

The *pharynx* is a musculo-membranous bag or pouch which opens at the back of the mouth, and grasps the bolus of food as it is presented by the tongue. Arrived at this point, its appropriate muscles successively contract and force onwards the pellet to the further end opening into the gullet. The food is now beyond the control of the will, and cannot be returned by any effort of a natural character.

The *œsophagus* or *gullet* is also composed partly of muscles and membrane. It forms an elastic tube reaching from the pharynx above to the stomach below, and occupies a position in the neck upon the left side of the lower portion. A knowledge of this fact enables us to trace the passage of substances throughout its visible course. The remaining part of the gullet passes through the chest, and is called the *thoracic* portion. The passage of food through the pharynx and gullet is termed *deglutition* or swallowing.

INSALIVATION.

The mouth is abundantly supplied with fluid for the purpose of lubricating its surfaces during motion in mastication. It also possesses peculiar solvent and chemical actions upon alimentary matters introduced, and thus effects special changes in their constitution, of vital importance to digestion and assimilation.

Saliva is the name given to this fluid, and is the produce of glands in the vicinity, the largest, the parotid gland, being placed below the ear behind the angle of the lower jaw. In addition there are others of a smaller character situated beneath the tongue, between the sides of the jaw, inside the lips and other parts; all of which separately contribute important properties to the fluids which mix in the mouth, whence they are conveyed by appropriate tubes or ducts.

The *solvent action* of *saliva* depends upon the presence of peculiar salts and a principle called *ptyalin* by scientific men, and is easily demonstrated by placing food within the mouth. It is also found to act efficiently when collected in suitable vessels and brought into contact with certain alimentary matters. Its power of altering the constitution of compounds is purely a *chemical action*, and is most peculiarly well marked upon those of a starchy character, abundance of which are found in the food upon which horses and cattle subsist. Through this influence they are converted into a principle called *dextrine*, and subsequently into *grape sugar*.

The salivary glands are under the control of the nervous system. In the human subject, the sight or smell of food of an agreeable character is sufficient to cause a copious flow to the mouth; hence the common expression "the mouth waters."

Saliva is secreted abundantly. The exact amount of this fluid which is formed is not easily obtained. A large horse is supposed to secrete 8½lbs. per day, an ox 102lbs. Mr. Hunting obtained half a gallon, or about five pounds in half an hour.

The *uses of saliva* are important and manifold. First, we have an abundant flow; second, its peculiar solvent power; third, its chemical action in converting starchy matters into sugar; fourth, its lubricating qualities during the presence of absorbing, or coarse and rough, substances; fifth, *it is secreted in major part during mastication, and continues as long as that act is carried on.*

This category of properties in a simple-looking fluid like saliva must have been conferred for a beneficial purpose.

We find such to be a law throughout nature. That purpose is essentially the primary step in rendering the component parts of the food assimilable, *i.e.*, converting them into constituent parts of the blood.

Being secreted at the time when the food is undergoing comminution between the teeth, it is presented at a period when it will be most effective. Food, therefore, which is swallowed quickly or greedily, without proper mastication, obtains little saliva, and the necessary transformations are not carried out.

It is impossible to supply a fluid artificially which can take the place of saliva. Mere saturation of the food by water does not promote digestibility as a consequence.

This has been satisfactorily proved many times. If the salivary glands are prevented from discharging their contents into the mouth during mastication, and water is thrown among the mass within the stomach, digestion is retarded. We have positive evidence of this in daily practice in those establishments where owners persist in using boiled mixtures of food, which is done in utter neglect of the most important fact that the horse has perfect grinders to crush and break down everything which comes in the way of *natural* food, with the best solvent immediately at hand, and in unlimited quantity, to effect a primary transformation towards the production of blood, bone, muscle, hoof, hair, &c. &e.

The practice is an attempt to set aside nature, and might be excused if none of the above appliances are present, or their capabilities in part destroyed. We are so accustomed to treat the horse by analogy, thus convicting him in the exercise of irregular practices, errors of body and mind in common with ourselves, that we naturally prescribed a mode of treatment based upon conditions supposed to exist.

Even a moderate acquaintance with the organized fabric of man and the higher animals leads to a different conclusion. It proves the practice unscientific, unsystematic, foreign, and *unnatural.*

I shall have more to offer upon the question of boiled food when a description of other organs has been given.

After the food has undergone the necessary processes of mastication and insalivation, and, as it passes backwards in the act of swallowing or *deglutition,* it becomes coated with a thick mucous or viscous secretion, thrown out from glands on the inner surface of the pharynx and gullet. It accumulates as the mass descends, and forms a thick greasy kind of coating, the proceeding having for its object mainly the avoidance of aggregation and stoppage in the gullet, a condition which under aggravated states constitutes choking.*

---

* It not uncommonly happens after hard work and long fasts, the horse, returning weary and hungry, ravenously swallows his

THE STOMACH.

Descending the gullet the bolus of food at length reaches the stomach, a pouch or dilatation of that tube. In the stomach further important changes are executed in the constitution of the food.

In man this organ performs the greater portion of the process of digestion. In the horse and ox but little analogy exists, and the essential points of difference will repay even a cursory examination.

The ox is endowed with four stomachs, or what is more in keeping with anatomical description, a quadrisect stomach, *i.e.*, containing four distinct compartments, each of which possesses different functions.

The first compartment is one of immense capacity. It occupies three-fourths of the abdomen, and is able to accommodate a great quantity of ingesta.

The second is small, and contains more fluid

---

food without due mastication and insalivation. The secretions are deficient by reason of fatigue or nervous depression and other causes. The bolus is speedily despatched, almost dry, and choking is apt to occur in its worst forms. If the food reaches the stomach aggravated colic is almost certain.

See my Prize Essay "On the Diseases of Farm Horses," published in the Transactions of the Highland and Agricultural Society of Scotland, Article—"Choking."

than the first, but both act in common in macerating and securing successive changes in the food.

The third exerts a degree of pressure, by means of its peculiar leaves, upon the alimentary matters arrested by it.

The fourth is the true digestive compartment, and resembles the stomach of man and the dog principally.

The ox is essentially an animal capable only of limited and not rapid exertion. The structure and arrangement of the digestive organs are clearly intended to accommodate large quantities of herbage of a mixed character, for which the functions are admirably fitted.

The horse, on the other hand, being made and required for rapid exertion, could not fulfil those ends with the digestive organs of the ox, and, therefore, like man and the carnivora, but one stomach or compartment is provided, which is both comparatively and relatively smaller.

The process of digestion is also wonderfully effective.

Whilst the ox has been known to retain food for upwards of six weeks within his stomach, little more than as many hours will suffice to ensure digestion in the horse. The process is, therefore, also wonderfully rapid.

The stomach of the horse, replete with food, acts as a great impediment to the action of the lungs, hence the great number of cases of *broken wind* and *chronic cough*, which are known to occur from irregular principles of feeding.

The horse cannot occupy himself in rumination or digestion almost entirely as the ox. He is required to undertake the removal of heavy loads, or otherwise engaged in rapid exertion. A rapid digestion in his stomach is therefore a very wise provision to relieve the lungs during action.

I have purposely exhibited substances of different degrees of solubility, and possessing a strong odour, to animals about to be slaughtered, and have been particularly struck with the fact that, in the short space of time which has elapsed between the administration of the medicine and opening the stomach, not a trace beyond the odour of the substance could be detected. The paper in which it was wrapped was usually found in the stomach, but the medicine had passed several yards along the gut, frequently within one hour.

Similar facts are observable with regard to food. I have known horses and ponies suddenly killed in coal mines by a fall of portions of the roof within one or two hours after a meal, and on examining the stomach it has been observed that digestion has progressed rapidly and effectively in that organ, only a small portion, the most indigestible, remaining behind. The more easily digestible portion had usually passed along the intestines in distances varying from ten to twenty feet or more.

It is a rule that all portions of greater solubility in the secretions, *i.e.*, more digestible, first pass out from the stomach in health.

Fluids also pass rapidly. They are usually carried to the cæcum, a large gut situate about twenty yards from the stomach in large horses, twenty minutes being usually sufficient.

These illustrations definitely explain why a horse occupies so much time consuming food. Put him into the stable after a day's work, and he will be found eating the greater part of the night. A small stomach, capable of effective and rapid action, is quickly emptied of its contents, and the desire for food, therefore, becomes almost constant.

We should gather from this also the absolute necessity of a regular supply of food, and abolition of long fasts and full racks and mangers when the animal returns to the stable.

THE INTESTINES.

The intestines are of two kinds, small and large. In the horse they occupy the greater portion of the cavity of the abdomen, and constitute the largest part of the alimentary track.

The whole length may be estimated at about ninety feet, or ranging from twenty-six to thirty yards.

The *small intestines* commence at the stomach, and in their course receive the several names *duodenum, jejunum,* and *ilium,* the divisions being purely imaginary.

About five or six inches below the stomach are the orifices which discharge the secretions of the liver (bile) and pancreas (a fluid resembling saliva). Besides these, other special fluids are poured from the walls (coats) throughout the length of the canal.

The walls are strong and provided with muscular fibres, as the gullet and stomach, to produce the necessary contractions (vermicular or worm-like) in order to subject the contents (ingesta) to the action of the various fluids, as well as cause it to pass onwards.

Throughout the inner surfaces of the small intestines a number of peculiar vessels are seen to enter. Their office is to abstract the nutritious elements of the food, which after meeting with the various secretions in the tube, assumes a whitish creamy consistence, and is termed *chyle*. The vessels here spoken of are termed *lacteals*. They communicate with other vessels and glands. In them the chyle as it passes onwards alters its constitution, and by successive stages assumes the character of the blood with which it is afterwards mixed. This constitutes the process of *assimilation*.

The small intestines are from fifty to sixty feet in length, and will accommodate from eight to eleven gallons of fluid.

The Intestines.

The *large intestines* of the horse are very capacious organs. The first, the *cæcum*, is a large conical pouch or bag, usually known as the *blind gut*. In it are collected principally the fluids drank, together with solid matters. The former occupy the extremity, the latter remain at the base. Absorption of fluids takes place from the cæcum in large proportion, and its contents are usually alkaline from the changes which take place in starchy constituents.

The *colon* is continued next in order to the cæcum. It is doubled upon itself, both parts throughout its entire length being united by intervening tissue, and traverses both sides and front of the abdomen twice, terminating in the rectum near the point from which it arises from the cæcum on the right side.

The cæcum and colon do not possess such thick muscular walls as the small intestines, but strong bands run longitudinally on four sides. These being considerably shorter than the intestines, have the effect of drawing them into puckers or folds, forming on the inner side a number of pouches, which assist in giving the characteristic form to the fæces or dung in the horse.

The *rectum* is very strong and muscular, but not so capacious, tolerably cylindrical, and terminates the alimentary track at the *anus* or fundament. Absorption from the large intestines is principally confined to the cæcum. The colon and rectum minister but little to that process. The *capacity of the large intestines* greatly exceeds that of the small. The cæcum will contain about four gallons of fluid, the colon about twelve, and the rectum about three gallons.

THE DIGESTIVE PROCESS.

The process of digestion is most complex and important, and deservedly receives an extended notice in all authentic works on animal physiology. It is impossible here to do more than briefly notice the leading stages, which are indispensable, but sufficient towards explaining generally the object for which these pages are written.

Gastric digestion.—In the stomach the food, already incorporated with the salivary and other secretions, is subjected to peculiar movements or contractions of the muscular walls, described usually as a "churning action." It is thus moved from one part to another and further incorporated with secretions (gastric juice) derived from glands (gastric glands) situate in the walls of the organ.

The *gastric juice* possesses acid properties, and a peculiar principle termed *pepsine,* which with the action of the stomach effects a reduction of the food to a uniform mass. The particles are in a fine state of division, and albuminous principles chiefly suffer chemical decomposition. At length the whole becomes a thick fluid and passes through the *pyloric* orifice of the stomach to the small intestines.

This fluid is called *chyme*. It contains nutritious matters in a state of mechanical suspension, others in chemical and simple solution, while a third variety are unacted upon from various causes.

Chyme proceeds along the intestines by virtue of the peculiar action of the organs. It first meets with fluids from special glands in the vicinity of the outlet from the stomach. Next with those from the liver and pancreas (sweetbread). By constant motion perfect incorporation is effected, and the following outline of changes may be observed :—

    1st. The acid character of chyme is neutralized—it is now alkaline.

    2nd. Albuminous matters escaping from the stomach unchanged are transformed.

    3rd. Starchy matters, unacted upon by saliva, are now effectually converted into sugar.

    4th. Fatty bodies are emulsified or converted into a kind of soap.

    5th. and lastly, all the nutritious principles have conferred upon them properties which facilitate their absorption and passage through the lacteals towards the blood, and the fluid mass now receives the name of *chyle*.

Chyle passes through the lacteals from the intestines. Its constituents gradually form a granular-looking mass, in which float a number of small vesicles or cells. By passage through an assemblage of bodies called *mesenteric glands*, the cells increase in number, and at length acquire colour, and eventually are poured into blood-vessels near the heart. It is thus the blood becomes the pabulum whence all tissues are nourished. In the elements of food are found the materials which, after assimilation, partake of the characters of the tissues of the body; and the circulation of the blood explains how each kind receives its share.

ELEMENTARY PRINCIPLES OF FOOD.

The chyle contains the whole of the elements of the food. These are of a mixed character. First, we have *nitrogenous*, so-called because they contain largely the gas nitrogen, or *albuminous* principles which are strictly the elements from which muscle is developed—hence the term "flesh formers" which is applied to them. Second, we have *fatty bodies* and *saccharine* or sugary principles—starch, gum, sugar, &c.—*heat-producers*. Third, there are essential constituents in the form of *salts*—of lime, potash, soda, magnesia, &c. Fourth, various *acids*, as hydrochloric (muriatic acid or spirits of salt), nitric (aquafortis), sulphuric (oil of vitriol), lactic and phosphoric, &c.

In a chemical point of view the acids are most powerful agents, and by union with various substances form compounds of vital importance.

Lastly, there are compounds of no service whatever to the system. These are principally indigestible bodies, such as ligneous or fibrous parts of plants and foreign bodies which have gained access to the digestive organs, cells, earthy matter, and portions of undigested food which have been present in excess. Liebig has termed these the incombustible and unburned parts of food. They are the refuse from the digestive process, and together with *effete* or useless parts thrown off from the system, constitute the *fæces* or *dung*.

ESSENTIAL CHARACTERS OF FOOD.

Certain conditions are essential for the proper digestion and assimilation of food. When properly understood, they indicate the principles of an economical system of feeding animals with a view towards the preservation of health and vigour under continued laborious exertion, as well as preventing an undue rate of mortality resulting from it, and at a low rate of cost.

These conditions are, first, that food should be nutritious; second, that it contains elements of a mixed character; third, that it possesses proportionate bulk; fourth, it should be regularly supplied; and lastly, the digestive organs generally must be in a state of healthy action.

It is imperative that food possess *nutritious principles*. This must be apparent from the fact that from it all parts of the body are built up and being constantly renovated. In order to possess this property, bodies rich in nitrogen are requisite, which are denominated *nitrogenous, azotised, nutritious,* or *flesh-forming compounds*. Examples of these are *albumen, fibrine,* and *caseine*—terms which would indicate different substances. Chemically, however, they are alike in composition, but exhibit physically different appearances.

If wheaten flour be placed under a stream of cold water a sticky paste is left behind. This is called *gluten,* and is identical in chemical composition with the flesh of man and animals. It is the nitrogenous or albuminous principle of wheat flour.

If an egg be broken a glairy fluid escapes from the shell, which becomes white and coagulates into a solid mass when heated. This is *albumen* —gluten in another form, identical in composition, and is the nitrogenous principle of the egg from which the flesh, feathers, claws, &c., of the bird are formed.

If milk is taken and an acid added, a solid mass of curds is speedily produced. This is *caseine*—or gluten, albumen, and fibrine in another form, supplied in the milk of the mother to young animals, and in peas, beans, &c., to older ones; from which also hoof, horn, hair, wool, skin, flesh, and feathers, &c. &c., are formed, developed, and repaired.

Lastly, if blood be coagulated, the mass which separates proves itself an identical compound to flesh itself—*fibrine*.

The whole then are the various forms in which the elements are conveyed to the blood, as found in the food upon which the animal subsists. By the action of vital processes within the system, each assumes those conditions which in themselves are vital. Their supply to the system must be constant in order to keep pace with the waste. Hence they are found abundantly in the food upon which man and animals live. Horses and cattle meet with them in the grass and corn which they daily consume, and man and carnivora obtain it directly by using the flesh and blood (fibrine) of animals as food.

The following table shows how these substances resemble each other in chemical composition:—

	Gluten from flour. Boussingault.	Caseine from peas. Scherer.	Albumen from eggs. Jones.	Ox-blood. Playfair.	Ox-flesh. Playfair.
Carbon	54·2	54·138	55·000	54·35	54·12
Hydrogen	7·5	7·156	7·073	7·50	7·89
Nitrogen	13·9	15·672	15·920	15·76	15·67
Oxygen	24·4	23·034	22·007	22·39	22·32
	100·0	100·000	100·000	100·000	100·000

NON-NUTRITIOUS PRINCIPLES.

In addition to the flesh-forming constituents of food, there are also needed others known as *non-nitrogenous, non-azotised,* or *non-nutritious,* so named in contradistinction to those which contain nitrogen. Examples are found in starch, sugar, gum, and fat itself. They are composed of carbon, hydrogen, and oxygen, *minus* nitrogen, and are found abundantly in the different varieties of corn and vegetables used as food.

Their services are required in the system equally with the albuminous compounds, but for a different purpose, *viz.,* the production of animal heat, and formation and storing up of fat within the system.

ANIMAL HEAT.

In order to render somewhat intelligible the principles upon which heat is developed, and maintained in the body, and the part which food plays in that process, attention must again be directed to facts.

Here it must be understood that although the term " heat producer " is applied to the saccharine principles of food, it by no means establishes an isolated fact. They are *not* the sole agents in the production of animal heat. I will attempt to explain.

Animal Heat. 33

To those who have studied chemistry, even but a little, the rapid development of heat unbearable in water previously cold is familiar. It is a good illustration for our purpose.

A quantity of cold water is taken in a tumbler or other thin glass vessel, and held in the hand, taking care to grasp that part in contact with the water. Sulphuric acid (oil of vitriol) is then added in nearly equal quantity, when by chemical action, which immediately takes place between the acid and water, intense heat is developed, rendering it an impossibility to hold the vessel in the manner adopted at the commencement.

The rubbing together of certain substances, or beating of metals upon hard surfaces, also produces great heat. Here the molecular disturbance—or the alteration of position of the ultimate particles composing the mass—which ensues from the concussion may not be unlike that which accompanies chemical action, although the means adopted to bring about each may be different.

It is, however, an undoubted fact that heat is developed by the chemical union of substances outside the body, and similar conditions are now found to apply to substances which are contained within it.

There are always met with elements and substances which, in contact with vital organs and their secretions, assume the power of union by chemical action. They pervade the whole of the

D

tissues of the body. All the actions essential to life are carried on at the expense of the materials introduced, and those which are present as ready formed tissue. Their formation and development are attended with the union and disunion of the elements of compounds present, and their waste or decay is likewise attended with the same results. Thus we have a general chemical action, and this accounts for the equal state of temperature throughout the body.

Under ordinary circumstances the saccharine principles of food are being constantly caused to assume the form of fat, which under passive states, or where little exertion is carried on, is stored up beneath the skin, between muscles and around various organs, giving the animal that appearance of rotundity so much prized when intended for the butcher.

If an animal in such a condition were caused to exert himself for any length of time, the fat is absorbed and consumed. Its consumption is an essential act, not only in maintaining animal heat for the purposes of warmth, but as an agent which facilitates the decomposition of other bodies intended for the use of the system, in a different manner. Such an animal becomes lean. His muscles are distinctly observed to be well mapped out beneath the skin. The same appearance is also brought out by illness or disorder, and is the process generally understood as "wasting of the body."

There are a number of animals, as the hedgehog, (hybernating,) which during the summer become enormously fat, and sleep throughout the whole of the winter. In this case, as no food is taken, the body maintains its animal heat entirely by the consumption of fat which has been stored up in the system.

The bear also disposes of himself nearly in the same manner. It is also a notable fact that our cattle lay on, during the summer, a great quantity of fat, which is derived from the plentiful herbage of the period. In both these instances we also perceive the provision which is ensured towards obtaining the necessary amount of warmth during cold weather, and when food is either withheld or not very abundant.

Animal heat is not maintained by saccharine bodies or fat alone. In carnivorous animals, as the lion, tiger and wolf, whose diet is confined to flesh, also the wild hunters of some countries who occupy their time chiefly in the saddle, sufficient fat cannot be obtained, nor are saccharine compounds forthcoming. Natural warmth then must be procured from another source.

Wild animals in their natural state, and the hunters of uncivilised nations, are on an equality. The habits of both necessitate much exertion—activity of muscle—and consequently waste or decay.

Flesh, upon which they live, being purely a nitrogenous compound, would furnish none of the materials for warmth under other circumstances. But under active work or movements, albuminous compounds are broken up, and the carbonaceous elements rendered available for the purpose.

A reference to the table at page 31 will explain how this can be permitted. In farther explanation it may be stated, that fatty or saccharine compounds are serviceable *only* for the production of heat as an adjunct to vital force; but nitrogenous compounds are capable, by peculiar action, of becoming not only useful for the manufacture of flesh, but also for the production of the necessary animal heat during exercise or work.

This explains why animals in high condition appear fresh and excited. There is a necessity for movement created in order to consume the highly nutritious material within the body. Wild animals confined to cages are seen to move about incessantly when awake. Here is another mode in which the system endeavours to appropriate the food, and bring about essential vital actions. Were it not thus, disease or death would be an early result, from an accumulation of deleterious principles in the blood, by which it is no longer able to support the body.

Man and animals consume little food when the body is covered by fat, and exercise but sparingly taken. The muscles are not developed because they are not used, in fact such a body is not capable of much exertion, by reason of that want of muscular development. It is neither so healthy, and is prone to disease in consequence of the absence of movements which promote vital action.

These facts are well known to practical horse owners, and they in consequence always avoid fat animals for immediate active work, and delay until the place is occupied by muscle.

We thus perceive that in feeding fatting animals and working horses two opposite principles must be carried out. It would be as absurd to feed a hunter or draught horse on the materials given to the cow or ox in the feeding house, as to expect they should replace each other in the scale of usefulness to man.

These facts dispose of the first and second propositions. We find that food is nutritious when it can minister to the formation and development of the body, and maintenance against waste; while substances of a mixed character are needed in order to keep pace with the requirements of the body in the production of a necessary temperature, and assistance in the accumulation of vital force.

Without materials specially provided for the latter process our working animals would be reduced to the condition of flesh-eating or caged wild creatures, with this serious disadvantage, the work imposed might act prejudicially, as it would not, in all cases, be so nicely proportioned as to suit the wants of the system, or when taken in accordance with the promptings of instinct in the creature itself. In short, food possessing elements exclusively of one kind, too rich in nitrogen, or too rich in carbon, at once proves insufficient to support life in a proper manner for any length of time. The experiments of Majendie and others who fed animals exclusively on one of the substances known as sugar, gum, starch, albumen, fibrine, or caseine, set this matter at rest for ever, and we are thereby taught that the animal economy can live and thrive only upon food provided *naturally*, and which contains *all* the elements calculated to minister to the tissues and functions of the body.

The poor inhabitants of Ireland, as well as the negroes of the Indies, also establish the truth of the principle. The former, who consume potatoes in large quantity, would exist in a poor degree of capability for exertion, were they not to add to this expensive and innutritious article of diet one of the compounds very rich in nitrogen, *viz.*, milk.

The coolies, who eat impure sugar, receive with it also nitrogenous compounds, gathered from the vegetable kingdom, and all the eaters of maize and rice resort to milk for the azotised principle, caseine.

Food, rich in mixed characters, supplies the necessary elements without disturbing the balance of the functions, which occurs when too much of one kind is given indiscriminately. All vegetable food is of a mixed character, but each kind differs in the richness of its constituents. A knowledge of this is of great value to all concerned in the keeping of animals.

BULK OR VOLUME.

Food should always possess an amount of bulk. Nature has not been unmindful of this when providing the nutritious principles of grain. The grain, or kernel, contains the nutrition in a concentrated form, and bulky material is to be found in the husk or stem.

Proportionate bulk is requisite to ensure digestion. The stomach cannot abstract nutrition from small quantities of concentrated food with benefit. The digestion and solution is not efficiently performed, as the stomach lacks the stimulus of contact, so essential to healthy action and secretion.

Grass, straw, and hay contain but little nutrition, and to ensure its abstraction, bulk is given to it consisting of water, ligneous matter (woody fibre), and salts.

The people of uncivilised nations have exemplified this from time remote.

The Kamschatdales mix earth and sawdust with the train oil they use as food, and in other northern regions a kind of bread is made from sawdust.

The natives of Ceylon use scraps of decayed wood with the honey consumed as food. Among animals the wolf is known to appease the sensations of hunger by taking into the stomach a great quantity of mud; the dog thrives best when he obtains his food from the ground, when it is mixed with grit and dirt, and in birds, small stones or sand is constantly being swallowed.

Food thus accompanied is fully compressed by the walls of the stomach, but when adventitious matters are not present, however nutritive, it does not fulfil the wants of the economy by virtue of its elements not being extracted.

ERRORS TO BE AVOIDED.

One of the great evils attendant upon the feeding of horses, and even cattle, is the use of *too bulky material*. By it the wants of the system are not satisfied, the stomach is over distended, and the process of chymifaction is retarded by the powers of the stomach being destroyed.

The walls are reduced in thickness, and rupture frequently takes place from the effects.

Fluids, however nutritious, as a rule, are not so easily appropriated as solid food. No better evidence is found than where cooked food is served to horses. The soft watery mass is too rapidly swallowed, and becomes as unnatural as it is innutritious.

It is an acknowledged fact that no process of cooking or preparation will render the food more nutritious, and there is positive proof that a mixture of substances, boiled to a pulp, are not so digestible as when given in a natural condition to working horses.

I do not expect that all who read this statement will be converted to the truth it proclaims. I am, however, certain that in the many places where the cooked system is carried out, there will be found persons desirous of successful reform and amelioration. To such I have great pleasure in addressing these pages. Others there are whom no amount of argument would convince, or practical demonstration convert. Bigotry, prejudice, and a stupid adherence to old customs have blinded them.

To change is considered unmanly, and, as existing affairs have probably prevailed for many years, unguided by either the light of reason or science, and having tradition only for their adoption and continuance, alterations would amount to sacrilege or disrespect to the blundering system which is worshipped with such folly and stupidity.

To resume. The stomach and intestines of the horse are not intended for sloppy food. The whole arrangement forms an assemblage of perfect organs eminently fitted for bruising, insalivating, digesting, and appropriating *natural* food, and unnatural slops and trash concocted by the device of man is attended with disease and mortality. Among horses, if we go no further than colic alone, the number of cases which occur where boiled food is used exceed those where attention is paid to the selection and supply of proper diet by *ninety per cent.*

Cooked food is open to grave objections. It weakens the digestive organs. It is swallowed rapidly, and the stomach becomes greatly distended, by which secretions are prevented or altogether stopped. Little or no insalivation takes place, and the food does not undergo those important and preliminary changes which have already been insisted upon. Secretions, otherwise necessary, are of no use with such an excess of fluid food, and if poured out are too far diluted. The stomach acquires in time an immense capacity and the muscular powers are weakened. The liver becomes diseased and the natural secretions very limited or absent. The intestines now suffer from this combination of results, and colic becomes of periodical occurrence, eventually ending in death.

The horses of many firms with which I am acquainted in Scotland, to whom boiled food is given, suffer very frequently from colic, and deaths are common.

Where proper systems are carried out, I have known three hundred animals belonging to one firm, doing the hardest work, kept in the best of health, and for a whole year not a single case occurs.

Mr. Hunting states that 120 pit animals under

his care, all in regular work, continued for six years without a single case of colic.

The bulk given to boiled food is looked upon by some as an advantage, and in illustration of the belief, a gentleman remarked recently that the food thus supplied to his horses must be more nutritious than other kinds, as it is softer, partially digested to begin with, and every twelve pounds put into the copper are increased to forty-eight. It must, however, be remembered that *thirty-six pounds of this is only water*. I would like to know who can conscientiously expect a horse to work well and continue in health on food which contains three hundred parts of water for every hundred of spoiled grain. It is an injustice to treat an animal in such a manner, which deserves more consideration on account of his usefulness, and whose better judgment would enable him to take water with greater comfort and benefit than can possibly accrue from deceiving him to swallow unlimited quantities in the form of a mess presenting such indescribable qualities and disproportionate quantities.

Cooked food for horses is a form which certainly has no analogy in nature, and wherever dictated, must inevitably arise from neglect or total ignorance of the anatomy of the digestive organs, with their physiology and the laws which govern assimilation.

To another objection raised against the cooked meat system, it is urged that horses so fed usually drink as much water as those confined to the dry meat or manger system. I believe there is truth in this as a rule, but the fact is not favourable to the plan, and great reasons may be assigned in the large quantities of common salt used in the mess, which occasions an unnatural thirst. Excess of common salt taken into the system proves highly injurious and predisposes the animal to disease, particularly of a congestive or low form, a condition of unnatural plethora being established.

The continued presence of sloppy food, besides acting—like bran mashes—as a foreign body, deranges the balance and harmony of vital functions generally, those of digestion primarily and particularly, and the large quantities of nutritious matter which may be present, having no admixture with natural secretions, are not rendered assimilable. *It therefore proves an expensive mode of feeding.*

Nutritious matters not having undergone those necessary chemical and vital changes which are ensured by the secretions of the digestive organs, are not in a fit state to enter the blood. They may be taken up, but will act as a foreign body there as they do to the intestines, and must be expelled or communicate disease.

If they remain in the intestines, diarrhœa is induced by irritative action, and horses so fed void their dung much like a cow. Such a state in this animal is not proper order, and if allowed to go on, disease of some kind supervenes.

On the other hand, if the unassimilated principle gains access to the blood, it is as soon as possible carried to the kidneys, and by them expelled. The animal frequently voids his urine. It will be frequently found to contain modified albumen, and even blood, and this accounts for the excessive number of cases of *diabetes* or *profuse staling* and *albuminuria* which have come under my notice during my residence in Glasgow.

Such cases are so common that they are considered trivial, and no doubt are, primarily; but when the errors of diet are allowed to proceed, they become marked by such characters as in the man wine-bibber and gourmand, or epicure, are modified, and appear as dyspepsia, biliousness, severe headache, piles, &c., a tolerable bloating of the countenance, with enlargement of the abdomen, which generally signifies organic disease.

The horse when suffering from these conditions is usually well drugged while at work, and as the same kind of feeding is persisted in, medicines repeatedly follow the aliment, the animal loses condition, and we may trace numerous instances of *farcy* and *glanders* to this as an undoubted cause.

Other terminations are dilated stomach, broken wind, congested, or scirrhous liver, calculi (or stones) in the intestines, recurrent colic, organic disease of the kidneys and bladder, or probably speedy death from over-distention and fermentation of the contained food, causing rupture of the stomach, some part of the intestines, or diaphragm (midriff).

ADVANTAGES OF PROPER FOOD AND SYSTEM.

My experience, and that of others who have devoted attention to the conditions discussed in the preceding section, clearly shows that the secret lies in *prevention*. This is comprised in cleanliness, ventilation, care and attention to the quality, quantity, and regularity of feeding, and due proportion of work.

The author is old enough to remember the effect of a journey from London to the north by stage coach, the character of animals selected for the work, and the amount they were required to perform. With such experiences he has frequently paused to enquire how the facts have failed to carry conviction in analogous cases at the present day.

In many of the coaches which ran between London, York, and Leeds, the horses were known to "do their fourteen miles out and the same number in" six days in the week. Their work was testified by the wear of the shoes, which, made of the toughest metal, and not unfrequently having an admixture of steel, were worn out by the fore feet in three weeks, and replaced on the hind by new ones nearly every fourteen days.

Notwithstanding this, by proper feeding, care, and ventilation of the stables, these animals retained their health and usefulness for years. Among them was a celebrated mare, "Old Sal." She ran in one of the above coaches as "off wheeler" for years, was known by all upon the road, had never been sick a single day, and when railways revolutionized the system of transit was over twenty years of age, and even then "as fresh as paint."

When the fly-boats plied between Glasgow and Edinbro' on the Forth and Clyde Canal, an old mare named "Maggie Lauder," was stationed to run between Port Dundas and Glasgow Bridge, a distance of eight miles, the time allowed being one hour. After a rest of one hour the return journey to Port Dundas was made, and in the afternoon she performed the whole distance over again, thus travelling and drawing the boat thirty-two miles per day.

The person from whom I obtained my information rode the animal daily for seven years, during which time she was doing the work alluded to six days in the week, "was never sick nor sorry a single day, nor ever had a day's rest in addition to the usual Sunday."

When the boats were superseded by railways, "Maggie Lauder" was sold at the age of *twenty-nine years*.

A similar instance is related of a horse employed in like manner on the Paisley canal. He was sold at the age of twenty-seven when the boats were discontinued, and, being "fresh as a lark" at the time, suddenly fractured the bone of one of his legs in his gambols while being led home by his purchaser.

I am aware that breeding will in a measure account for "pluck" and disposition to work in animals as well as in man, but it will not stand in the place of *ability* under any circumstances. The willingness or pluck may be always present, but ability will depend upon a condition of strength.

One thorough-bred horse will resemble another very much in disposition, but differ widely in ability from mode of living. Take the first from the green pasture and run him alongside that brought direct from hard dry corn and sound hay, upon which he has subsisted months, and performed daily exertion. The effect is easily perceived; weight or distance is scarcely an object to him, but the first is blown or lamed before half a dozen fences are crossed, or has received his death summons from various causes.

Harness horses, and horses used in draught, require similar treatment to produce strength and endurance.

While pluck is derived from breeding, strength is derived from food and a healthy digestion. Corn and hay, transmuted within the penetralia of the living organism, becomes muscle. Manure, the refuse of digestion and the animal body, the agriculturist knows, nourishes his land, without which he can expect no crop. In the production of artificial light, all depends upon the supply of combustive material and agents which support or promote the process, which, in proportion to quantity and quality, afford a good or bad kind of illumination. In the warming of buildings the maximum temperature can only be obtained by instituting an operation of the laws of combustion upon materials capable of undergoing that process, and likewise, by the operation of laws within the animal organism, if we need strength (force), it must first be supplied in the shape of sound, dry provender.

There is a very erroneous idea, at least to my perception, entertained by many, that where a draught horse is required for moving extreme weights he should be large and ponderous. If the dealer is inquired of, " You want weight," says he. If a friend be appealed to, a similar recommendation is given. It is in this way many useless, heavy-legged, unsightly, lugubrious, and slovenly animals are tolerated. What these are supposed to gain by superior capabilities in moving weights they lose in speed, and hence are seen creeping along the streets, and, as occurs in some towns, creating quite an obstruction to general traffic.

It appears to me that strength is required, not absolute weight, but a good development of muscle. If weight only is wanted, it would not be so frequently remarked that horses " will not pull a sitting hen off her nest."

And, again, if nothing but weight will suffice, then a lump of lead or any inanimate object would answer equally as well.

I would refer my readers to Youatt's excellent treatise on draught, and they will perceive that other objections are against tall animals for moving loads, particularly on four-wheeled carriages.

REGULAR FEEDING.

It is one of the essentials of good management that horses should receive their food as regularly as possible. Without regularity, and especially with long fasts, the digestive organs are prostrated or weakened, and food, which would otherwise be nutritious, brings about those changes already described.

In coal mines, where feeding and work is dictated by those who know nothing about it, broken wind, colic, diabetes, organic diseases of various kinds, calculi, and death by rupture, are common. When, on the contrary, attention is given, these fatalities are rare, and when they occur are usually traced to other causes.*

---

* Much valuable information has from time to time been detailed to me by my friends, Mr. Charles Hunting, M.R.C.V.S., and Mr. Luke Scott, M.R.C.V.S., whose experience in the management of pit animals is of the most extensive character in Britain, and therefore to be received with respect.

CALCULI OR STONES IN THE INTESTINES.

The nature and aggregation of the particles which compose these bodies are not without interest, as affording information on the conditions which are present in the stomach and intestines. *Calculi* are very common in the horses and ponies of some coal mines, and also among the horses of millers, general carters, and those used in large establishments where the system of feeding and work is defective.

Their origin is usually considered to arise from water impregnated by the salts of lime, which are precipitated in the same manner from solution as occurs in the steam-boiler or tea-kettle.

It does not follow that calculi form on the use of such kind of water. It is also a most notorious fact that from water of precisely the same character supplied to the animals in two coal pits, different results are manifest. In one, where proper care in feeding and work is observed, there is the greatest amount of health, but in the other, where systems are the reverse, and especially when work is excessive and irregular, calculi exist.

That the water draining from the magnesian limestone, and holding lime in solution, has not much to do with their formation, is proved by several circumstances.

First: Many calculi which I have found in

such animals have little or no lime in their composition, being mainly composed of mucus, hair, dirt, coals, &c., closely matted together, and known as *"dust balls."*

Second: The miners consume large quantities of the same water, but are not known to suffer from intestinal calculi.

Third: From personal experience and residence in districts where calcareous or hard waters only can be had, I have ascertained that calculi are not more prevalent when system is observed; and

Fourth: I have found calculi to exist more abundantly where water is of the purest character. Some of the largest specimens which have been obtained were from horses using soft water alone, and therefore must have another origin.

To attribute their formation to any special kind of water is a false theory, and negatives the power of the intestines to remove useless matter.

The presence of a nail, piece of wood, stone, or other hard substance, is also said to insure the formation of calculi. But horses and cattle meet with these things constantly among their food, and, while many are doubtless rejected by the sensitive lips, others are swallowed, as proved by their presence in the dung during life, or intestines after death.

The *origin* of the material which forms the substance of a stone or calculus is undoubtedly from the *food*. Hard waters may assist under certain circumstances.

They may contain a large quantity of lime, but the food relatively contains a much larger proportion. It is a substance largely in demand for the wants of the system.

If the animal is enfeebled by overtaxing work, long fasts, and supplied with food of an inferior quality, a condition known by the term *bulimia* is established. This is known by an irregular, capricious, and morbid appetite, irregular bowels, staring coat, leanness, inaptitude for work, and a desire to lick the walls. Sometimes, however, these symptoms are either not well marked, or escape observation.

Under such circumstances the animal swallows sticks, stones, and rubbish of all kinds, to appease the ravenous desire within. Food, under these conditions, is not properly digested, the secretions are vitiated, or altogether deficient, and act imperfectly. Farther derangement occurs, in which the liver particularly suffers, and affairs now assume an aggravated character.

During these conditions assimilation and absorption is not carried on perfectly, and the mineral matters of food and water are deposited in the solid form, and aggregate around any rough surface or object which may be present.

As the mass increases in size corresponding derangement is continued, and thus secures material for its development, or the formation of others—as many as fifty having been found in one animal.

Some time may elapse before acute symptoms are observed. Suddenly abdominal pain arises. Symptoms are continued, and become aggravated, admitting of no relief, and the animal dies.

Upon making a *post-mortem* examination, one or more of these stones are found to have passed into a narrow part of the gut, and become imprisoned by spasmodic action of the muscular walls which tightly enclose it on all sides. Sometimes destruction of the gut has occurred, and the stone is partially or wholly liberated along with the contents of the intestines.*

OBJECTIONS TO THE USE OF DRY FOOD.

It is urged by many persons enthusiastic in the feeding and management of horses, that a change

---

* I have succeeded in obtaining a great number of these interesting specimens during the past sixteen years. In less than two years twenty-six were obtained from pit animals, having caused death, and many more were found in animals dying from other causes.

Their composition was principally mucus, the felted down from the oat, silicious matter and carbonate of lime. The last-named substance usually formed the outer portion, while the interior was filled by pieces of coal mixed with the other ingredients. Many of these were presented to the museum of the Albert Veterinary College, London.

Several fine specimens have recently been forwarded to me by my friend, Mr. Thomas Foreman, M.R.C.V.S., Leadgate, Durham, exhibiting similar peculiarities. Of these he has collected a great number from pit animals.

to a system of bruising and cutting of food gains only one advantage—*viz.*, the animal fills his stomach quicker, and is thereby enabled to take more rest.

This property is pre-eminently claimed in favour of cooked food, and in addition, that it is partially digested for the animal. Experience and systematic inquiry prove the fallacy of these tenets.

I have shown that digestion, when properly carried on, is wonderfully rapid and effective.

The stomach, being small, is rapidly emptied again. This obtains in all horses, including those fed on the *manger system*.

Every one knows the effects of bran mashes. How much more, then, must constant supplies of food, supposed to be half digested at commencement, containing much water, and being an unnatural mixture, act like a foreign body?

The laws of the animal economy render such results inevitable, for as quickly, in proportion, as the stomach is voiding the digestible portions, the sensation of hunger arises, and desire for food is appeased by taking in more. Thus it will be found, in opposition to the argument in favour of a half-digested food, that the process of digestion is accelerated, and more is required. Such food always fails to give up the whole of its nutrition; *the animal eats more, costs also more, and gains the least by the method.*

It is thus that an equally long time is occupied

in the consumption of food, and visit him at any hour of the night, he will be found having an appetite, and like Oliver Twist "looking for more."

Rapidity of digestion is a provision established by nature. If the stomach had been from the first intended to receive the large quantities frequently placed before horses, or to perform functions assigned to the teeth and salivary glands in addition to its own, the logical inference is that, as nature, in her development of all things, has not studied ornament merely, the stomach would have been endowed with greater capacity and powers, and teeth and salivary glands in all probability absent entirely.

It is also urged against the dry meat or manger system, that horses fail to masticate or grind the whole of their corn, that much in a state capable of germination or growth passes out in the excrement, and, of course, the cooked meat system supplies this deficiency.

During a season of extreme scarcity in India, it has been stated,* the famine-hunted wretches followed the English camp, and drew their principal nourishment from the grains of corn extracted from the excrement of horses.

I well remember an extensive firm employing many horses, whose manure was objected to by

---

* Letter from an Indian officer to J. Curwen, M.P., quoted in Blaine's (fifth) edition of "The Veterinary Art."

several farmers because they obtained crops of oats in places where they were not required, after using it on the land. I have also observed the heap of manure literally covered with green blades from the growing oats. How was this, and why has such a simple circumstance had no better effect than to induce a system of porridge feeding for an animal eminently unfitted for it?

It was in this wise. The remedy was sought for in a manner too superficially; and in the absence of an acquaintance with the principles of management, the horse has been compelled to suffer for the omissions of others.

In such cases I have known carpenters, and even more unlikely men appealed to for information and a remedy. The system resembles very much that so commonly adopted under certain Acts of Parliament, where discretion and power is given to tailors, joiners, bailiffs, policemen *et hoc genus omne*, to pronounce in a magisterial court what is cruelty to animals in a medical point of view, and to descant upon the pathological signs which prove a carcass to be diseased, and all this in the teeth of an educated scientific witness.

Such matters require dealing with philosophically. They are not within the comprehension of every clodhopper, groom, and coachman, who fancies he knows all about a horse because he cleans him. Their duties lie in the practical administration of the brush and broom, and faithful execution of all orders entrusted to them. Management and dictation form no part of these.

The internal arrangements of the horse and all domestic animals require the assistance of brains not so illiterate, and if they were properly supplied with such, the horse and his master would enjoy a much longer acquaintance.

It is important to us to inquire whether oats or any kind of grain are capable of growing after having passed through from eighty to ninety feet of intestines subjected to healthy acid, alkaline, and other peculiar juices which convert their starch into sugar, separate and modify their albumen and caseine, and dissolve out salts, or to a temperature varying from $98°$ to $102°$ F., occupying time varying from ten to twenty-four hours?

I venture to predict not, and to assert that very few grains will pass out unacted upon. If such were the case the whole processes of mastication, insalivation, digestion, and that of making malt are but a farce, and cannot be accounted for by the present deductions of science.

The solution of the growing oats, however, was soon made apparent.

The manger system had been imperfectly carried on for some time without any alteration in the size or character of the mangers themselves. These were shallow, narrow, and not provided with cross-bars. In this way much was wasted by the horses throwing out the corn when searching for better portions.

In addition, I entered the stables on one occasion when the premises were supposed to be deserted, and observed a number of those young urchins who are always a kind of *sine qua non* about lorries and stables, carrying on a mimic warfare, the missiles in the case being oats, obtained from the open corn-bin or granary. It was afterwards ascertained this had been a common practice. The successful remedy soon followed in the shape of deep and wide mangers, with iron cross-bars, padlocks to the corn-bin and granary door, and institution of a proper room for mixing the corn and cut food.

That the half-famished Indians picked something out of the excrements of the horses I have no doubt, and they most probably resembled oats in appearance. Birds, especially sparrows and common fowls, are also captivated to make such a selection for their crop. But only in outward appearance would these abstracted matters resemble the grain of oats. Few have trusted themselves and their judgment in troubling in this matter farther than making the broad assertion on the strength of appearances. A superficial mode, and very delusive proposition to be circulated. I have tested the matter and found it to be an error.

If the stomach and digestive organs generally are in a state of health and order, very few grains escape their action, and the common inference is that if the horses of the Indian campaign referred to really parted with so much corn as to support such a number of followers, they must have been fed in a very imperfect manner, their digestive organs in a state of disorder, and from the loss of the food, in a condition certainly not desirable in an enemy's country.

In France the subject met with the attention of Boussingault and Papin, who instituted experiments, and ascertained correctly that the passage of undigested grain from the bowels of horses in health is merely nominal.

Out of eight pounds allowed per diem only one ounce of unchanged grain could be detected, and this weight included moisture.

The digestive organs generally should be in a state of healthy action in order to secure the proper benefit from food.

Under this head there requires little to be written. I have fully shown how disease originates by false management, and how waste occurs in food supplied under such circumstances. It must, therefore, be apparent that those organs specially set apart for providing the fabric of the animal body should not be overtaxed or enfeebled. If such occurs the whole body suffers more or less.

Care is especially needed after protracted hard work and long fasts, avoiding the use of large quantities of cold water upon the contents of a well-filled stomach, or supplying too much food at one time. In fact these precautions would repay, if followed, at all times; neglect of them is a frequent source of derangement, and from which fatal consequences usually succeed.

Where a great number of horses are kept it is far more profitable to employ a person whose sole occupation is confined to the feeding department. Corn, &c., should be transferred to his possession under proper rules for mixture and use, the quantities being accurately stated in documents handed to him. In return he should furnish evidence of having carefully complied with the terms, and his papers should also afford particular information as to consumption under all circumstances, regular or variable.

He should be a man who will carefully notice the condition of all horses when brought to the stable, and willing to minister to their comfort in properly regulating the quantity of food each may receive without injury.

The details of such management require special attention in order to be properly applied to the various circumstances which obtain in different establishments. There is, however, no particular difficulty beyond a willingness that need be encountered, in order to make the whole safe, satisfactory, and profitable.

In the absence of particulars it would be an

impossibility to attempt to lay down a plan suitable for any particular establishment. An outline must be framed on the principles here given, the work, size, and nature of animal, &c., being points of importance for consideration.

PART II.

VARIETIES OF FOOD.

The food used for working horses are those cereals and leguminous seeds which, usually denominated corn, consist of oats, barley, Indian corn or maize, peas, beans, and tares, together with hay, straw, bran, and linseed.

These vary much in their properties as well as nutrition, and on that ground alone arises the question, "What kinds are best, and what proportion should be given?"

An answer will greatly depend upon circumstances, such as the character of work imposed, together with the market price and condition of the provender.

The relative proportions of nutritious matter contained in different kinds of food have been ascertained from time to time by analysis, an outline of which is as follows:—

In 100 pounds.	Nutritious matter.	Fat, or heat producers.
Turnips	1	9
Red beet	1½	8½
Carrots	2	10
Potatoes	2	25
Hay	8	68½

In 100 pounds.	Nutritious matter.	Fat, or heat producers.
Maize, or Indian corn	12	67
Oats	14	68
Barley	18	$68\frac{1}{2}$
Bran	18	4
Linseed	24	$64\frac{3}{4}$
Beans	31	$51\frac{1}{2}$
Peas	32	$51\frac{1}{2}$
Tares, or lentils	33	48

Maize or Indian Corn.—By the above table it will be observed that maize among corn contains the least percentage of nutritious matter, and from it we gather that it is not suited as a principal article of diet for working animals. It contains a great proportion of water and starchy matters, and forms in consequence an excellent food for pigs and fatting animals, given with other varieties.

Oats stand next in proportion, and by custom have been most commonly selected as a principal article of diet for horses, but prove very expensive as sometimes used. This is very apparent on calculation, and results are demonstrative in practice.

A horse doing little work, or what actually only amounts to exercise, would be economically and advantageously fed upon hay and oats, as the demand for muscular power not being great, such articles form a very suitable diet, without causing him to become overloaded with fat and a burden to himself.

Varieties of Food.

Estimating oats to weigh 42lbs. per bushel, and costing twenty-six shillings per quarter (eight bushels), the cost per week for different allowances, together with the amount of nutritious matter contained, would be somewhat as follows:—

Pounds per day.	Pounds per week.	Cost. s. d.	Azotised or nutritious matter in pounds.
10	70	5 5	9·8
12	84	6 6	11·76
14	98	7 7	13·52
16	112	8 8	15·68
18	126	9 9	17·64
20	140	10 10	19·60

In addition, sixpence must be added for each stone (14lbs.) of hay consumed, which yields 11·20 oz. of nutritious matter.

Oats should be heavy in the hand, devoid of thick husks, and short and plump in the kernel. Good dry potato or Scotch oats, weighing 39 to 42 pounds per bushel, are undoubtedly cheapest to purchase at all times, and to be preferred to other kinds weighing from 33 to 37 pounds, even when four or five shillings extra per quarter is paid.

It is no saving to purchase corn, especially oats, *made up* to a certain weight. Some dealers guarantee four bushels of oats for a stated price to weigh, say 160 pounds, and when measured the quantity considerably exceeds the four bushels.

Under such circumstances the purchase cannot be as beneficial as if the oats were 160 lbs. natural weight. The inference is, the grain is of an inferior quality, the kernel being light and the husks disproportionately heavy. *It is always more profitable to obtain standard measure and weight,* as this proves an important item in twelve months, and particularly when animals are doing variable work.

The lower priced oats may answer well for moderate exercise or work, but as soon as the labour is increased, or a change is made from standard weighing oats to others of a lower nutritious percentage, animals suddenly fall away in condition, and become liable to disease, and in ignorance of the real causes, are not unfrequently impregnated with a course of useless and even dangerous drugs. It is thus the expenses of feeding are obviously increased, as to them are to be added less ability for work, and an additional incurring of expense, while the original cost of the provender is really but a fraction below the price of good material.

When the kernel of oats is small the husk preponderates, the former containing as low as eight per cent. only of nutritious matter, and the latter no better than straw itself, but for which the price of oats is paid.

Mr. Hunting proved this by a set of tedious

but ingenious experiments. He says,* "One ounce of foreign oats, 39lbs. per bushel, was weighed, the same weight of old Scotch, 40lbs. per bushel, and the same weight of Tartar oats 36lbs. per bushel. The foreign oats contained 1,112 kernels, the Scotch oats, 1,084, and the Tartars, 1,144. The husks were weighed. The husks of the 1,144 grains of Tartars weighed 120 grains; of the 1,112 kernels of foreign oats, 126 grains; while the husk of the 1,084 kernels of Scotch only weighed 96 grains."

Under these circumstances, horses fed upon three bushels of oats per week, weighing 42lbs. per bushel, would receive 126lbs. total weight, of which 25lbs. would be husks, having a value only of four per cent., in nutritious matter.

Change this to Tartar oats at 39lbs. per bushel, exactly 39lbs. must be extracted for husks, and if the foreign oats are used, 36lbs. would be the amount of husk in the same quantity.

It must be borne in mind that the inferior kinds of oats are not only remarkable for a preponderance of husk, but their nutritious matter, and consequently their feeding qualities, are considerably below the standard weighing Scotch oats.

Similar rules should be applied to other kinds of grain or corn, and their standard qualities

---

* "On the Feeding and Management of our Domestic Animals," p. 14.

obtained from analyses upon which reliance can be placed, and information will thus be easily obtained whereby to institute a system of mixtures for any purpose of feeding.

SELECTION AND PURCHASE OF GRAIN.

Most persons are aware that corn should be thoroughly dry for feeding purposes, otherwise inconveniences occur in the form of indigestion, colic, weed, grease, or loss of condition, &c.

Besides, in purchasing that which is not dry, or seasoned, a decided loss occurs, which buyers should avoid by securing a reduced price in accordance.

Owing to this, large feeders take advantage of the markets, and purchase oats, peas, beans, barley, &c., as they are aware that in good corn the loss by a reasonable evaporation of water is an ample payment for the construction of granaries for spreading out and constantly turning; added to which, animals are kept in better condition, and work is less interfered with by illness on that account.

I have known hundreds of quarters of corn purchased under such conditions, and with the observance of other measures, to be noticed, a balance has been shown which has cleared the cost of keeping the animals for a great portion of the time, as compared with the previous cost from another mode of feeding.

The purchase of grain should not be referred to week, month, or year, in fact, to no period if it can be avoided. It is much better to store up corn and ensure it being thoroughly dry, than to depend upon purchase when it is immediately required. Many good bargains are put in the way of owners who are open to purchase, and the profit obtained helps to improve the appearance of the credit side of the balance sheet.

Where roomy grain floors cannot be had, it becomes a matter of greater necessity that the provender should be dry, and of *guaranteed weight and measure*. Of a necessity also, a higher price must be paid for it, and even under those circumstances it answers far better than the use of inferior kinds. To constant purchasers, dealers are to be found who will endeavour to provide what is required in the shape of a regular sample, and thus difficulties are greatly overcome.

These principles have been more understood of late by those who feed large numbers of horses, and whose competitive kind of work requires them to study every item of expenditure. In some instances animals are fed inexpensively, and preserve their health and condition with remarkable benefit from the system, even under much harder work.

ECONOMY OF FOOD.

The method of economizing food consists in using *a variety of grain* instead of one kind, and that exclusively oats. Some have tried the different leguminous kinds also separately, but found them inefficient in economy, and even injurious.

A farmer of my acquaintance having about thirty horses, purchased, at a cheap rate, a quantity of Indian corn, under the idea that it would effect a saving in the cost of feeding. On the contrary, the health and condition were greatly sacrificed.

Others, again, give a preponderance of beans, acting upon the well known fact that, being more nutritive than oats, they must be more economical. In the mode adopted, however, they have proved highly expensive as well as injurious.

Linseed is also added, and with pernicious results. It is too laxative for general use in quantity, but judiciously administered proves assimilative, hastens the process of assimilation, and assists in the formation of fat and flesh. As a nutritious body it is very highly expensive.

Tares, which are the most nutritious diet we can use for horses, are objectionable as being unpalatable in quantity. Similar objections may be urged against other varieties of food when exclusively used, particularly in their liability to produce disorder of the digestive organs.

A mixture, therefore, should be regulated by special conditions. Due consideration is to be given to the nutritious matter contained in each ingredient, and as a whole, the amount and character of the work, quantity allowed to each animal, and the price paid at the time. Where the consumer is compelled to go to the dealer for his week's, fortnight's, or month's supply, this is particularly needed, as there is no room for speculation on the rise or fall of corn, upon which frequently large sums are to be saved.

In estimating the amount of nutritious matter contained in food of different kinds, and how much is required to preserve horses in health under their work, the table given in pages 63, 64 will be found of great service. Practically, it is answered by observing the quantity of oats of standard nutrition, or other kind of food, which may be required to keep the animals in condition for work and perfect health. The amount of nutritious matter is then determined according to the per centage stated opposite each kind by simple rule of three. This done, the estimate of nutrition contained in other kinds is observed, and mixtures arranged, forms of which will shortly be submitted.

It is to be next inquired, will this ensure a less cost than is incurred by the principal use of oats? The answer is emphatically, yes, and with a greater supply of nutrition.

I am indebted to a gentleman of great experience among horses for valuable information in the feeding of his animals.

They are employed in the town of Sheffield, which is not unlike Glasgow for its hills.

The work is severe, and consists in removing the heavy manufactures of steel, stoves, hardware, &c., to and from the railway station. Drays or lorries are generally used, and three tons is a common load.

In a letter to me dated April 4th, 1864, he says:—

"Our horses' diet is as follows:—

Hay	16 pounds per day,	8 stones per week.
Oats	10 ,, ,,	5 ,, ,,
Beans	5 ,, ,,	2½ ,, ,,
Maize	4 ,, ,,	2 ,, ,,
Bran	2 ,, ,,	1 ,, ,,
Total	37 ,, ,,	18½ ,, ,,

No loose hay, all is chopped; oats, beans, Indian corn all crushed separately, then the whole is mixed with the chop. The hay costs 4s. per cwt., oats, 1s. per stone,* maize, 11d., beans, 1s. 2d., and bran 7½d. per stone.

"I always buy of the best quality without regard to price, as I find that the cheapest, all points considered. As a rule, I greatly prefer English oats.† The harvest of 1862 was an

---

* The hundredweight is 112 lbs., the stone 14 lbs.
† I think the term English is here applied without prejudice

exception, and I bought foreign oats principally, being in a superior condition to English. In addition to the above—which is the winter scale, the summer is somewhat reduced—we every Saturday night give each horse a mash of linseed mixed with a small proportion of bran, boiled altogether and given warm.

"This serves to lubricate and clear the bowels, and comforts the animals. I do not know whether that is the cause; but since its adoption we have had few, if any, cases of colic, or severe inflammation; prior to the adoption of that system these cases were of great occurrence."

It must be borne in mind that these are heavy horses, and we have here also an evidence from an unprejudiced source, that a considerable amount of nutritious matter is required to keep up the health and condition of the animals, since when the inferior kinds of mixture were supplied, in the shape of oats principally, disease was common. This I can testify, having been in professional attendance.

We are also taught practically that a loss of condition and proneness to disease is brought about by food containing too little nutrition, when the demands upon the system are excessive.

---

to Scotch oats, but as a distinction to foreign and inferior kinds. The writer is keenly alive to the qualities of the various kinds of corn, having had unlimited experience in the feeding and management of the best draught horses in large numbers, and doing the hardest work.

Suppose these animals had been fed exclusively upon oats and hay, they would require to consume weekly *four-and-a-half bushels* of the former, and about *ten stones* of the latter, in order to receive the same amount of nutrition— viz., 31½ pounds derived from the mixture quoted, and which would cost at the same prices about *eighteen shillings and sixpence.*

Here is also a decided saving of three shillings and sixpence per horse per week, by the use of the mixture, which only costs *fifteen shillings*, and with fifty horses would realize £8 15s., and for a year £455, besides almost an immunity from disease and death, to which they were before exposed.

SYSTEMS ADOPTED ON VARIOUS COLLIERY ESTATES.

It is by paying particular attention to these matters that so much has been effected in the saving over former expenditure, on many colliery establishments, where the supply and mixing of grain is under the management of the veterinary surgeon.

Mr. Hunting, in his pamphlet already referred to, has shown that with the number of horses and ponies employed at the various collieries of the South Hetton Coal Company—all doing the hardest work—the saving effected in ten years amounted to no less than the enormous sum of

£31,876 2s. 7½d. by cutting the hay into chaff and mixing with small quantities of straw, and substituting superior kinds of beans, peas, barley, tares, &c., in lieu of oats. He also states that out of 225 horses employed in two pits, during six weeks between 15th December, 1850, and 24th January, 1851, when the old system was pursued, there died of colic and its consequences *three horses and ponies;* while with the same number of animals under the improved *régime* during seven years, there were *less than three cases per annum.*

CUT FOOD AS AN AGENT IN PROMOTING PROPER INSALIVATION.

The value of this kind of provender as an agent in causing a proper insalivation of food is undoubted. On this subject Mr. Hunting is as explicit as he is full of information regarding it. He found that a number of animals, all selected as near as possible with an average age, height, and common appetite, required much longer time to consume the same weight and measure of food cut and mixed in the manger than when it was given in the shape of long hay in the rack, and oats only in the manger, from ten to thirteen minutes more being required.

After what has been said in reference to the objects of the teeth and salivary glands and their secretions, it must be obvious that in giving food in its naturally dry state, it serves more important uses in the animal economy. And as the *quantity* of saliva plays also an equally important part, the use of cut food is here unmistakably shown to be a very desirable proceeding.

At the *Helton Colliery*, Mr. Luke Scott, M.R.C.V.S., has followed out most useful principles. His attention had been arrested in 1851 by the inefficiency of the existing system of feeding, and proneness to mortality which was constant among the horses and ponies employed.

The quantities allowed per pay * to each animal employed in connexion with the estate were as follows:—

	Oats in Bushels.	Cost. £ s. d.	Hay in stones.	Cost. s.	Total. £ s. d.
Waggon Horse	8	1 6 0	28	14	2 0 0
Farm Horse	6	19 6	20	10	1 9 6
Pit Horse	6	19 6	24	12	1 11 6
Pit Pony	3	9 9	12	6	15 9

It is necessary to state, the whole of the hay here allowed was not consumed. Much is constantly wasted in collieries by being carelessly sent down the pits, or conveyed to the stables in large trusses, which come in contact with water, dirt, and grease. The animals consequently refuse it, and generally place it beneath them, sufficient being

---

* Colliery accounts in the county of Durham are made up once a fortnight, when wages are paid; hence the term "pay."

frequently gathered to make a very good bed. I have seen a week's supply of hay and corn lying exposed to the dust flying from the pit mouth, as well as steam, condensing as it falls from the boilers, and, in common instances, to the rain of one or two nights in addition, before being sent down. The former kind of unsystematic arrangement was of frequent occurrence at one pit, but no kind of remonstrance succeeded in effecting an alteration.

Pit animals are usually kept *twelve hours* at work, and in many cases, *without food and water,** or at least without a satisfactory amount of either, and seldom periods of rest.

I have known animals kept from their stable thirty-six hours at a time, and when complaints have been made they have been met with a stout denial from the powers that be; or, where denial has been useless, it has been assigned as a cause, that the veterinary surgeon has not provided a sufficient number of animals for the working of the pit, an office which he does not include among his duties without express orders.†

Such long fasts act very prejudicially upon

---

* The practice is not so common as formerly. In some pits it is abolished, but slumbers in others.

† Lord Kinnaird, in his letter to the Home Secretary on the Fearndale Colliery explosion, dated 15th November, 1867, has fully shown the aspect of colliery affairs when he quotes the words of the miner, who says, "If people as knows dared to speak, these things would soon be stopped."

the animal. When he returns to the stable the food is seized and ravenously swallowed, and, as a consequence, it does the least good, but is more frequently productive of the greatest harm.

By a reference to previous remarks on the estimate of nutritious matter in the various articles of food, it will be found that the Hetton Colliery "old plan" of feeding was doubly expensive and extravagant. It was innutritious as it yielded to the waggon horse (and others proportionately) one-fourth less nutriment than the mixture given hereafter. It was expensive because it cost nineteen shillings per week, from its use much was wasted, the animals were in bad condition, and mortality great.

It was decided, at length, to allow Mr. Scott to regulate the system, which he did, in the following way:—

His first act was to have the hay cut in trusses of sufficient size to fit a coal tub,* in which they are sent down the pit, and thus totally prevented from collecting dirt and grease as before. This resulted in a saving of the amount wasted, and also supply in a better condition, which would be turned to account in the animal body.

The varieties of grain fixed upon to be used were bruised separately, and mixed in the following proportions:—

---

* This plan is also carried out at all the collieries under Mr. Hunting's superintendence.

Cut Food in Promoting Insalivation.

Grain.	Weight per bush. lbs.	Price per qr. s.	Actual weight. lbs.	Cost. s.
Barley, 4 bushels	56	30	224	15
Oats, 4 "	42	26	168	13
Peas, 2 "	66	40	132	10
			524	£1 18

In order to arrive at an average number of animals to be fed, the ponies and horses in the pits are classed as follows :—

All above 15 hands are called horses.

Three above 13 hands, and under 15 hands, equal to two horses.

Two above 11 hands, and under 13 hands, equal to one horse.

Under this arrangement the whole were reduced to an average of 130 horses.

The superiority of the system is at once apparent by a reference to the subjoined analysis, in which the two plans are contrasted.

Old System, for One Pit Horse.

6 bushels of oats per pay, at 3s. 3d.	19s. 6d.
24 stones of hay, at 6d.	12s. 0d.
	£1 11s. 6d.
Or for 26 pays (one year)	£40 19s. 0d.
Nutritious matter contained	52·08 lbs.

New System, for One Pit Horse.

176 lbs. of the mixture	14s. 4d.
18 stones of hay, at 6d.	9s. 0d.
21 pounds of bran	11d.
Total per pay	£1 4s. 3d.
Or for 26 pays (one year)	£31 10s. 6d.
Saving effected for one horse for one year	9 8s. 6d.
Cost per horse under old plan	£40 19s. 0d.
Saving in 130 horses for one year	£1225 5s. 0d.
Nutritious matter contained	48·18 lbs.

In the old system it will be observed that 52·08 lbs. of N.M. (nutritious matter) are contained in the food supplied, against 48·18 lbs. in the new. The greater part, however, was not obtained by the animals on account of the excessive waste already mentioned in the hay, and from the greedy manner in which the corn was devoured.

The additional 4 lbs. of N.M. supplied also proved expensive, besides useless, as it was unavailable. For it the sum of 7s. 3d. per pay was being paid, as forming part of a system which engendered disease, and gave the animals even less support, although professedly, a mode which furnished a large amount.

It is now a custom to allow the pit animals a portion of the hay and corn during the day, instead of causing them to fast twelve hours, as before.

The result is, Mr. Scott has found that the food is more leisurely taken, masticated, and thoroughly digested.

Besides the saving effected in actual expenditure, the reduction of disease and losses by death, is an important item. In repeated visits to the animals in the pits fed upon Mr. Scott's principle, it is due from me to state that I never saw a greater uniformity in condition while the hardest work was being imposed, and cases of indigestion, colic, and death in consequence, were the exception, and of extremely rare occurrence.

WHAT CONSTITUTES A CHEAP FOOD.

It is usually considered a cheap mode of feeding, when material can be supplied for one penny per pound, and I find several owners base their calculations of cost at this rate. But it must be borne in mind that food costing only one penny per pound is not inevitably an economical food. We must look farther than mere cost. Economy does not consist in price alone, to such must be added the veterinary surgeon's account, whose services in the main will be found to have been occasioned by the supposed economical food, and in addition, the value of the amount wasted by refusal, fermentation, or that which is hastened through the bowels in the state of "partial digestion," so much insisted upon.

Again, the amount of nutritious matter contained must be accurately calculated, or no reliable estimate of cheapness can be made. I am aware of several large firms in Glasgow who believe they are feeding economically upon one penny per pound rates, while their food yields ten per cent. less nutrition than the preceding mixtures, and cases of acute indigestion, &c., &c., are constant and numerous. These form a good comparison with the systems of Messrs. Hunting and Scott, the mixture proposed by the latter costing only ninety-eight parts of a penny per pound, with a high scale of nutritive value.

OBJECTIONS TO A CHANGE OF GRAIN.

It is frequently urged that to adopt a total change in the kind of grain used, is to produce serious evils and fatal disorders, as exemplified by animals gaining access to the open corn bin, or to a heap of wheat or barley, when either rupture of the diaphragm, stomach, or intestines takes place, and death speedily ensues, while at other times founders (laminitis) occurs.

These certainly appear grave objections at first sight, but in reality are difficulties of no moment. We are speaking of *systematic* feeding, *not* deliberate engorgement. Death or disease results in one case by repletion and fermentation consequent upon the bolting of an unnatural quantity of food, which, if taken under proper principles, would in the other prove nutritious and life supporting. The death of horses by these means is fully carried out in analogy among mankind, with the exception that in the latter gluttony generally exerts itself a little more slowly.

In no case, with proper caution, will evil consequences ensue by a change to the dry, or manger system, from any other. It need therefore cause no apprehension.

NATURE, USES, AND ABUSES OF BRAN.

Bran will be found by analysis to contain from 14 to 18 per cent. of azotised matter, equal in fact to oats or barley. In nutrition, however, it is inferior to the straw of wheat or barley, a property which appears to obtain with the husk of grain generally. Owing to some peculiar form of combination, the azotised matter is not liberated by the process of digestion; hence those who consume bread in which the bran of wheat has been retained, under the idea that such is more nutritious, are greatly mistaken. The fæces or excrement are loaded with bran which has passed out almost unchanged, and horses fed upon it exhibit the same conditions.

That an admixture of bran with wheaten flour

or with the provender of horses, is useful and even profitable, there can be no doubt. This is to be attributed to the mechanical action set up by the silicious particles, which obviates constipation, and preserves the proper action of the digestive organs when given in a judicious manner. Messrs. Hunting and Scott take advantage of this property, and use it *daily* with their superior mixtures of corn.

As *a laxative*, bran is justly called into requisition periodically as a warm mash for animals in whom there exists an innate disposition to constipation. I place the action of a bran mash, *given occasionally*, as one of the safest, most natural, and acceptable adjuncts towards the preservation of health; which effect is produced with more benefit and less deterioration to the system than by any other means. There are few horses that will not take it when offered as a change, and I would recommend, especially in winter, that it be given at the temperature of new milk, *not cold*, and the use of it should not be insisted upon indiscriminately, or ill effects are speedily shown.

Nothing can be more anomalous than the opinion entertained on the use of bran, as it obtains in many quarters. Believed to be non-nutritious, it is given largely during disease, to ward off critical inflammation, which a diet of corn might increase, but why it is persisted in with animals suffering from general prostration and weakening complaints is quite paradoxical.

It too often occurs also, when no appetite exists, it is paraded continually before the creature, and lies in the manger fouling the wood-work by fermentation, which the animal shows his repugnance to by standing as far back as his chain will allow.

SYSTEM PURSUED AT THE LONDONDERRY COLLIERIES.

The horses and ponies employed at the collieries of the late Marchioness of Londonderry (now Earl Vane's), during my appointment as Veterinary Surgeon to her Ladyship, and subsequently for a short period to the Earl, were fed upon oats and peas—five parts of the former to one of the latter. The mixture was, however, never regulated by weighing. It was quite of an extemporary character, and entire guess work, a dash of peas being hastily put into the bottom of a "*poke*," and afterwards covered to the top with bruised oats, and the *whole* then weighed. In addition, hay, and green food in summer, was allowed, the cost of which I find by returns in my possession, amounted to £1 3s. 10½d. per horse per pay, all ponies being classed as two equal to one horse.

Under this arrangement 106 horses and 322 ponies exclusively employed in producing coal, and of course below ground principally, would in round numbers give 267 horses, the cost of feeding each being £31 0s. 9d. per annum.

At first sight this appears, and is really believed to be a very economical rate of feeding, being lower than Mr. Scott's expenditure at Hetton-le-hole. Quality, however, is the test of cheapness, not the price alone at which the food is supplied. This allowance yields not more than 37·52 pounds of nutritious matter—assuming the one part of peas are carefully added, which I have grave reasons to doubt—against 48·18 in Mr. Scott's feed, in which 10·66 lbs. extra are supplied each pay per horse during the year, for which he incurs a cost only of 9s. 9d., the difference per horse per year.

But, as in the case of the old system at Hetton-le-hole, the animals do not derive the whole of even this limited amount of benefit from the corn allowed. In winter *steamed food*, consisting of hay, linseed, and the one-fifth part of peas abstracted from the mixture, are supplied. This is sent down the pits during the afternoon, and frequently before the animals reach the stable in which the mess has been deposited by the horsekeeper, I have found it undergoing fermentation. Some, in fact many, of the animals refused it even when fresh, and from these causes the most nutritious portions were lost to them.

The process of steaming was conducted at separate places contiguous to a number of collieries, and the food conveyed in boxes or coal-tubs placed in carts, and throughout the distance a dark-coloured fluid drained in profusion, of course carrying with it some of the most useful soluble principles of the food.*

The process of steaming food may answer well where inferior food and hay abound, cattle are to be fed, and aged dependants require some light employment. But as applied to good food, and carried out in the manner alluded to, it is a complete farce, a useless addition to expenditure —which, by the bye, is not made to appear in connexion with the feeding—and deprivation to the hard-working animals. In fact, the whole system of feeding is no better, hence the number of cases of colic and indigestion, rapid falling away in condition, diabetes, &c., &c., which occur, and not being required to be reported at headquarters nothing is known of them. But if the gentlemen who attempt to feed horses without visiting them at their work or in their stables, and others who rule with pens and ink in a comfortable office, had to ride off at all hours in all kinds of weather three, six, eight, or ten miles, descend a coal-mine, remain in the heated atmosphere several hours, and take the place of their coachman *outside* the conveyance in the cold night air, after influences equal to a severe

* In a visit to a large estate owned by a noble earl, where feeding is supposed to be conducted upon scientific principles, steamed food forms a large item for cattle. After the process is carried sufficiently far the food is removed, and the fluid accumulated from the condensed steam, containing useful soluble matters, is allowed to drain away in the gutter, while the animals are supplied with water for drinking. *Cui bono?*

vapour bath, each would perceive the advisability of reform. As such irregularities are in a coalpit hundreds of feet below the surface, they *do not see*, and it is very useful to be *determined not to see*.

With the exercise of common knowledge a man may be expert at purchasing corn, and make good bargains, but it requires a little more than that to adapt a proper system to the constantly varying wants of a large number of animals. If the principles of dieting and management require no more philosophy, and can be conducted with success without presence or information, the sooner such gentlemen take up also the treatment of disease by a system of telegraphy the better, and probably they may then make both ends meet still more satisfactorily to themselves.

From a strict examination of all phases and conditions, as they exist on that estate in common with many others, a more highly nutritious diet can be guaranteed—a reduction of disease and mortality therefrom to a minimum by the exercise of care and watchfulness, and these with a saving of *hundreds of pounds annually*.

The principle is of easy calculation. In large numbers, say three or four hundred animals, if two or three shillings only per week can be saved, it is a large sum at the end of the year. With other agencies it may also be increased. But on collieries there are objections to figures, except when they are used by the powers that be, and reports, although desired, are as waste paper. Like the phœnix, however, these may rise from their ashes, and, under another name, with an official envelope, appear as new and *original* creatures altogether.

In leaving this part of the subject, I would inquire how it is possible for a pit horse of fifteen or sixteen hands, with his large muscular system—doing from twenty to thirty miles a day, drawing a train of coal tubs, one way empty the other laden with many tons, in a highly heated and dusty atmosphere, and perspiring freely—to obtain sufficient nutriment from an allowance of twelve pounds of oats per day. The same is allowed to many carriage horses, and those of our cavalry regiments receive it within a fraction, for which exertion amounting to healthy and necessary exercise only, compared with the work of a pit horse, is exacted.

OTHER FORMS OF ADMIXTURE.

I have shown that nutritious mixtures of corn may be used with great advantage at a low cost. Their use and application should be guided by existing circumstances.

Animals should be selected as much as possible from an average class, character, and age; but an intelligent overlooker would soon be able to perceive, even among a mixed class where any differences existed, and modification is required.

Some would need a little more food than others —particularly aged ones—while there are others whose assimilative powers being more active, would derive more nutrition even from a little less food, and thus spare a trifle to their less endowed neighbours.

In the studs under the care of Mr. Hunting at South Hetton, Murton, Rhyhope, Trimdon Grange, Seaton Delaval, &c., &c., and Mr. Scott, in the old Hetton Collieries, animals of all ages are to be found, and, by the system carried out, are equally well provided for.

If, owing to the severity of the work, a more nutritious diet is called for, it will be found in the forms as follow, which provide it at an equally cheap rate.

Mixture No. 1 (Low rates).

		Weight.	Cost.		
		lbs.	£	s.	d.
Peas	4 bushels	264	1	0	0
Barley	4 ,,	224		15	0
Oats	3 ,,	126		9	9
Bran*		98		4	1
		712	£2	8	10

This mixture, divided among seven horses during one week, would allow each over 14½ pounds per day, at a cost of 6s. 11¾d., out of which 20·14 lbs. of N.M. (nutritious matter)

---

* The nitrogenous principle of bran is not calculated in these mixtures for reasons stated on page 83.

would be obtained. Divided among six horses, each would cost 8s. 1½d., and obtain 23·63 lbs. of N.M.

Divided among five horses, each would cost 9s. 9d., and obtain 28·36 lbs. of N.M.

Mixture No. 2.

		Weight. lbs.	Cost. £ s. d.
Peas	4 bushels ..	264	1 0 0
Barley	4 ,, ..	224	15 0
Tares	1 ,, ..	67	5 4½
Oats	1 ,, ...	42	3 9
Bran	....	98	4 1
		695	£2 8 2½

Divided among seven horses, each would receive over 99 lbs. per week, costing 6s. 10½d., and obtain 21·65 lbs. N.M.

Six horses would receive 115¼ lbs. each, costing 8s., and obtain 25·26 lbs. N.M.

Five horses would receive 139 lbs. each, costing 9s. 7½d., and obtain 30·31 lbs. N.M.

Mixture No. 3.

		Weight. lbs.	Cost. £ s. d.
Peas	4 bushels ..	264	1 0 0
Barley	4 ,, ..	224	15 0
Tares	2 ,, ..	134	10 9
Bran	....	98	4 1
		720	£2 9 10

Divided among seven horses, each would receive over 102 lbs. per week, costing 7s. 1¼d., and obtain 23·86 lbs. N.M.

Six horses would receive 120 lbs., costing 8s. 3½d., and obtain 27·84 lbs. N.M.

Five horses would receive 124 lbs., costing 9s. 11½d., and obtain 33·40 lbs. N.M.

It must be borne in mind that good hay yields five per cent. of N.M. which must be added to the above for the quantity used.

It will also be observed that peas are named in the foregoing mixtures to the exclusion of beans. They are not so productive of constipation as beans, which on that account enables us to use them with greater freedom. Beans are, however, unobjectionable when used with oats and bran, chaff, &c., in sufficient quantities. Prices must regulate these mixtures from time to time, due consideration being paid to the N.M. contained in the various kinds of grain.

When the prices of grain are much increased, such mixtures as the following must be taken, and will be found adequate at an equally low cost.

From the *Field* of 21st September, 1867, we learn the prices current at Mark Lane were, for oats, 35s.; barley, 43s.; peas, 43s.; beans, 44s. per quarter of eight bushels, and tares, 7s. per bushel. Bran cost at that time 6s. per cwt. of eight bushels.

Mixture No. 4 (High rates).

		Weight. lbs.	Cost. £ s. d.
Peas	6 bushels	396	1 12 3
Beans	4 ,,	264	1 2 0
Tares	2 ,,	134	14 0
Barley	1 ,,	56	5 6
Bran		112	6 0
		962	£3 19 9

Divided among twelve horses, each would receive 80 lbs. per week, costing 6s. 7¾d., furnishing 21½ lbs. N.M.

Eleven horses would receive 87½ lbs. each, costing 7s. 3d., and obtain 23½ lbs. N.M.

Ten horses would receive 96 lbs. each, costing 7s. 11¾d., and obtain 25¼ lbs. N.M.

Nine horses would receive 106½ lbs., costing 8s. 9¼d., and obtain 28½ lbs. of N.M.

Eight horses would receive 120 lbs. each, costing 9s. 11½d., and obtain 32⅛ lbs. of N.M.

Mixture No. 5.

		Weight. lbs.	Cost. £ s. d.
Beans	4 bushels	264	1 2 0
Peas	4 ,,	264	1 1 6
Tares	2 ,,	134	14 0
Oats	1 ,,	42	4 4½
Bran		112	6 0
		816	£3 7 10½

Ten horses would each receive 81½ lbs., costing 6s. 9½d., and obtain 21 lbs. N.M.

Nine horses would each receive 90½ lbs., costing 7s. 6½d., and obtain 23½ lbs. of N.M.

Eight horses would each receive 102 lbs., costing 8s. 6d., and obtain 26½ lbs. of N.M.

Seven horses would each receive 106½ lbs., costing 9s. 8¼d., and obtain 30½ lbs. of N.M.

Mixture No. 6.

			Weight. lbs.	Cost. £ s. d.
Beans	4	bushels	264	1 2 0
Peas	4	,,	264	1 1 6
Barley	3	,,	168	0 16 1½
Tares	2	,,	134	0 14 0
Bran		,,	112	6 0
			942	£3 19 7½

Twelve horses would receive per week each, 78½ lbs., costing 6s. 7½d., and obtain 19¾ lbs. N.M.

Eleven horses would receive each 85¾ lbs., costing 7s. 2¾d., and obtain 21½ lbs. N.M.

Ten horses would receive each 94 lbs., costing 7s. 11½d., and obtain 23¾ lbs. N.M.

Nine horses would receive each 104 lbs., costing 8s. 9d., and obtain 26 lbs. N.M.

Eight horses would receive each 117¼ lbs., costing 9s. 11¾d., and obtain 29¼ lbs. of N.M.

Seven horses would receive each 134½ lbs., costing 11s. 4¼d., and obtain 33¾ lbs. of N.M.

The present prices of grain, &c. (February 1871), afford the means of suitable contrast with the foregoing. By using the following mixtures, actual cost need not be increased.

Mixture No. 7.

		Weight. lbs.	Cost. £ s. d.
Peas	8 bushels	504	2 0 0
Beans	4 ,,	252	1 6 0
Barley	4 ,,	200	0 15 0
Oats	4 ,,	152	0 12 0
		1108	£4 13 0

Fourteen horses would receive 79 lbs. per week, at a cost of 6s. 7¾d. each, yielding 21 lbs. of nutritious matter.

Thirteen horses would receive 85 lbs., at a cost of 7s. 2d., yielding 22¾ lbs. N.M.

Twelve horses would receive 92¼ lbs., at a cost of 7s. 9d., yielding 24¾ lbs. of N.M.

Eleven horses would receive 100 lbs., at a cost of 8s. 5½d., yielding 27 lbs. N.M.

Ten horses would receive 110¾ lbs., at a cost of 9s. 3½d., yielding 29¾ lbs. N.M.

Mixture No. 8.

		Weight. lbs.	Cost. £ s. d.
Peas	8 bushels	504	2 0 0
Barley	4 ,,	200	0 15 0
Oats	4 ,,	152	0 12 0
		856	£3 7 0

Ten horses would receive 85 lbs. per week, at a cost of 6s. 8¼d. each, yielding 21 lbs. N.M.

Nine horses would receive 95 lbs., at a cost of 7s. 5¼d., yielding 24 lbs. N.M.

Eight horses would receive 107 lbs., at a cost of 8s. 4½d., yielding 27 lbs. N.M.*

It remains only to be added that by a careful estimate of the prices of grain and leguminous seeds, together with the relative amounts of nutritious matter contained in each, it is possible to vary the mixture in such manner as the foregoing, that, notwithstanding the excessive fluctuations of markets, the cost of each animal per week for corn will not vary throughout the entire year more than a few pence.

The bulk will, however, be somewhat less, and requires to be made up by the use of hay, or hay and straw chaff.

As these mixtures are designed for hardworking animals only, it will be almost unnecessary after what has been said when speaking of animal heat, &c., to state that such food will prove pre-eminently injurious to idle animals, except given in very small quantities. To those doing no work or light exercise, oats are decidedly the safest article of diet.

---

* In feeding horses upon oats alone, weighing 38 lbs. per bushel, costing 24s. per quarter, each must consume 5 bushels weekly, at a cost of 15s., in order to derive the same nutrition as here afforded by a mixture of 27 lbs. per day, at a cost of 8s. 4¼d. per week.

GREEN FOOD.

Among hard-working horses, I have found the use of green food too indiscriminately adopted, and it frequently proves as injurious as a mass of cooked food.

That it is useful and beneficial I fully believe, but this occurs under proper management. When given, it should by no means take the place of corn. This is, however, too commonly done, the animal being allowed too much.

He then perspires freely, becomes weak and liable to disease. I have known for years that among town cart and cab horses to whom grass has been allowed as described, sore throats and influenza have appeared almost simultaneously with its use, besides colic, weed, &c., &c.

Two or three weeks' feeding while the plants are young may answer for easily wrought horses, but in my opinion that state of the animal's body which we term condition should not be so trifled with. Aptitude for work is not a condition which is obtained in a few days or hours. It is only obtained during weeks, and at considerable expense. Most persons know, or at least presume to know, what training the racer requires, and how long a hunter is in being got ready for the field; yet we find the same people sacrifice the condition of a draught horse during a season when he requires the greatest strength, by the supply of an innutritious and watery food.

I maintain, if horses are in condition and required for work, that green food is an interruption to the formation and maintenance of muscle, and it should be avoided. If he requires rest, green food will be serviceable; and, like his more favoured master, he should be allowed a trip to the country, where, in a roomy loose box or covered yard, he can enjoy the green fruits of the earth, which are regularly mown and brought to him, protected from the rays of a scorching summer sun, or the pelting rains that fall, and flies which torment at this season.

When these conditions are not fulfilled, green food proves expensive and unprofitable. The animal loses condition and is below the standard for work, while he becomes peculiarly liable to disease, and exhibits the greatest difficulty in taking on flesh, appearing lean, hide bound, and generally betokening want of power and activity.

Similar remarks apply to the use of turnips or carrots. Moderately used raw in winter they prove serviceable—in excess they are positively injurious.

ECONOMY OF USING CHAFF AND BRUISED CORN.

With regard to the bruising of corn and cutting hay into chaff, I find the practice attended with good results. It suits a mixed class of animals better, and causes a more perfect mixture of each kind than would be derived from the food in the whole state.

It is an important proceeding where boys are employed; for where they have access to unbruised corn, they often take out beans, peas, or tares for pigs, rabbits, poultry, or pigeons at home.

The cutting of food, as already shown, causes a proper and continued flow of saliva—an important process, in order to ensure digestion of the numerous starchy elements of food upon which horses and cattle live. The cost* incurred is very little with proper machinery, and amply repays for the outlay in a very short time.

By the addition of *oat* or *wheat-straw*, a saving is not only effected, but the food is further aided in digestion. The usual proportions are one-fourth straw and three-fourths hay, but many persons use equal parts.

These are strictly non-nutritious agents as used. They are given purposely for providing

---

* It is frequently estimated that hay costs 2s. per ton cutting, and the bruising of corn one penny per bushel. Mr. Hunting, however, informs me that the work is performed at the South Hetton colliery for half these sums.

necessary bulk, and assisting in grinding down the other portions of food within the digestive organs. As an agent of nutrition hay is very expensive, and in that respect little superior to straw, which, with other food, I have known given regularly to animals, no hay being allowed, while the condition has been all that could be desired.

In all the cereals and leguminosæ ripeness of the plant is evidenced by the development and perfection of the seed in the various receptacles; prior to that stage the stem contains the nutrition. Notwithstanding this fact, so apparent as it must be to every farmer that the analogy exists in each, hay is allowed to stand for days, and even weeks, before being cut, when it must be an utter impossibility for any increase to take place. Growth is completed, the plant ripens, as indicated by the seeds becoming plump. They contain all the nutriment, and in the main are shed upon the ground by every wind that blows, leaving the hay nothing better than a fine sample of straw.

The higher price asked for this fine sample, we may infer, is to cover the loss occasioned by this species of neglect.

I wish it to be understood that I am not prejudiced to the exclusive use of cut hay and bruised corn. When given whole these substances may be effectively masticated, and the animals will appear excellent and pay well for the proper selection and mixture of food. I, nevertheless, consider that a larger profit accrues by *avoiding the waste* which always happens when hay is given whole (or long), besides suiting for general purposes much better.

Food so prepared will require *wide and deep mangers* fitted with cross bars, to prevent the animals throwing it out in their search for the more tasty portions.

On this subject many investigations have taken place at home and abroad, and the results are, without exception, favourable.

In France, Leblanc found that animals fed upon boiled food fattened, but lost vigour and became affected with disease; while dry food had a contrary effect. M. Charlier says, with cooked food the animals are very subject to disease, but since the regular adoption, by omnibus proprietors, of dry, bruised, and cut food, founder, colic, and illnesses generally, which each week were numerous, had become quite exceptional.

PEA AND BEAN STRAW.

The question has frequently been put to me, "Is pea or bean-straw useful for feeding horses?" To this an affirmative answer may be given, when the article has been carefully gathered and housed. It should always be cut up small, and mixed with the bruised mixtures of corn, and large quantities should be avoided by using with it cut hay. Equal parts of hay and pea-straw, or three parts of hay to one of bean-straw, will answer very well for working horses, but I deprecate filling the racks with either.

The many fatal cases of disease which occur from their use, is owing to the inferior condition of the straw, coupled with being in undue quantities and other irregularities, which too often exist in the farm stable.

SAVING TO BE EFFECTED.

Carefully carried out, these principles will effect an enormous saving, and I have no hesitation in stating that, among the numbers of animals employed in Glasgow and other large towns of Great Britain, it may be raised to *thousands of pounds annually*, and, in addition, a corresponding sum by the avoidance of disease.

The farmer need not grudge his horse corn, since it can be shown that he can be fed at less cost than many now incur on inferior hay, straw, and provender generally, and derive greater aptitude for work.

The poor man may also feed better and save a few shillings weekly, which would be well applied to the formation of a fund wherewith he could replace his animal in the event of death, without resorting to the subscription system over his immediate district, which is too commonly done.

The principles are important to large owners, who might also raise a fund with the savings for the same purpose, and to remunerate, in some cases I could name, those who are able, and study to apply effectually the system calculated to bring about the change.

All food should be of the best quality and kind. If inferior kinds are purchased, and require disguising by some process to make them palatable, the sooner he who purchases such is removed the better.

No mixture or process of doctoring can render such available as nutritive food when the elements are not present, nor can any admixture of condimental nonsense effect it either. The experiments of Mr. J. B. Lawes have definitely proved that when animals improve their condition with the use of condiments—which in themselves have no nutrition scarcely—the result occurs from an *increased consumption of corn.* The proprietors of such compounds may state what they please in puffing their wares. But against their puffing it can be positively asserted, as an undoubted fact, that condiments, spicy foods, or by whatever term they are known, do not effect any improvement upon inferior food with which they may be mixed, and are not economical, as set against common salt, which is far superior at one-fortieth the price. On the other hand, they are expensive articles of diet, and can only be looked upon as substances quite dispensable, and of no great service in the feeding of animals.

Within a recent period a sample of food intended for working horses, cattle, and sheep, has been submitted to me by Messrs. Whyte and Cruikshank, Chryston Mills, near Glasgow, which, although bearing the name of a "Patent Prepared Food," it is only justice to state, partakes of none of the qualities of condimental or spicy foods. It is a preparation embodying, to a certain extent, the principles laid down in these pages, the whole of the ingredients being carefully selected, decorticated, ground, and baked. It is highly spoken of by several proprietors, and will doubtless prove a great boon to those who cannot devote attention to the selection of provender for horses, or where only one or two are kept. I, however, have no experience of its use, but judging from information received as to its composition, and the respectability of its inventors, have no doubt it will fulfil the ends claimed for it, and call for an extended trial.

IMPORTANCE OF GROOMING.

There is one particular in the management of horses which so materially influences the effects of food upon the system, that it will not admit of being unnoticed, although the attention be exceedingly brief. This is *grooming*.

Importance of Grooming.

How far this principle is carried with many of our town dray and cab horses can be clearly ascertained by merely passing within a few yards as they stand in the street. After they have spent hours in the open air, the odour of the stable is yet strongly upon them.

There are, doubtless, good reasons to be assigned for this in some instances, the most common being that of absolute laziness. There are, however, cases where a groom or horsekeeper is expected to execute multifarious duties in addition to those of the stable, and in consequence the horse is neglected. Another fruitful source of neglect is to be found in low wages, and the men endeavour to make up the deficiency by looking after per-centages.

Therefore it proves to his interest to be careless and incur expense upon all sides, which is done to an alarming pitch in some instances. A third cause is the unreasonable number of horses which are placed under the care of horsekeepers. This is a most monstrous practice in some of the coal mines. I have found it to occur invariably, that where the animals are working in the greatest amount of heat and dust—two or even three miles from the bottom of the shaft—where they perspire most freely, and endure every vicissitude inimical to general health, there they have had the least attention.

All this arose from an excess of duties.

In such cases I found men having the care of

almost a fabulous number of animals, and the only reasonable conclusion one can come to is, that such work and conditions are imposed upon the poor creatures, that it would amply repay the Society for the Prevention of Cruelty to Animals, and other adherents to Martin's Act, for an application to Parliament to institute special investigations into their condition, with a view to an amelioration. For less than one-twentieth—ay, one-hundredth—of the physical appearances of a pit animal witnessed in a horse in our streets, the keen eyes of the policeman would have a case, but from these places in the recesses of the earth there comes no cry, and nothing is known.

One horsekeeper had under his care fifteen horses and nineteen ponies; a second, four horses and twenty-four ponies; a third, twenty-three ponies; a fourth, two horses and thirty-eight ponies; a fifth, nine horses and twenty-eight ponies.

Three men had the care of five horses and eighty-nine ponies in a sixth instance, and three others had the care of twenty-two horses and fifty-one ponies.

These animals are to be fed, harnessed, and cleaned to go out to work at 5 a.m. by these men, who descend several hours previously in order to attempt an impossibility.

If we take the mean of these numbers, we shall find that each man had an average of thirty animals to attend to. The arrangements

Importance of Grooming. 107

of the stables are not always suited towards reducing the labours of the men, being frequently in a continuous line of stalls arranged on one side, which necessitates several journeys to each animal for turning to water, tying up, supplying with corn and hay when they cannot be fed at the head. Estimating the trouble which these men have, and the risk they run for a few shillings a week, one cannot be surprised that the horses and ponies do not receive their proper share of attention.

The idea of cleaning them is estimated as the boy did the operation of washing his hands and face when he refused on the score of their becoming as bad again shortly. Such an estimate, however, does not render the fact as it exists less flagrant.

Let each man be limited to a specified time for the execution of the various details expected from him, and it will be more apparent how absurd must be the belief that these animals can obtain one-fourth the necessary attention under their peculiar and extreme conditions.

Feeding with corn, each one minute	=	30 minutes.
" hay, "	=	30 "
Harnessing, with repairs, two minutes	=	60 "
Turning to water and tying-up, one minute	=	30 "
Brushing down, each five minutes	=	150 "
Which occupies for thirty animals or five hours in all.		300 "

The men descend at 2 a.m., which only leaves *three hours* to perform a number of duties, the time for which, estimated as low as possible, is not sufficient to allow of their being effected in any other than a most slovenly manner—really occupies two hours more than the men can actually bestow on them. At night they are merely stripped, watered, and fed, in order to allow them rest.

To occupy more time with them would be also prejudicial, as the hours of rest would be materially interfered with; and consequently an average of thirty animals, estimated at about £300, are thought no more of than to value their care and management at the rate of fifteen shillings a week, or sixpence per head—the amount paid to the horsekeepers.

Here, where the truth of the old maxim, "A good cleaning is equal to a feed of corn," would be faithfully realized, it cannot be carried out.

When complaints were made, and exact conditions represented, all was pooh-pooh'd, and any alterations it was said would cost the estate £300 per annum, as ascertained by figures, which, emanating from the executive were reliable, but worth nothing when they arose from the mental calculations of one who was not a "Viewer."

Such is the connexion which exists between the skin and digestive organs, that if these poor creatures could receive a guaranteed dressing of fifteen minutes only, each night and morning, the effects would be marvellous.

In a solitary instance, one man had fourteen animals under his care. As he was infirm and contented himself solely with the employment as horsekeeper, he could devote more attention to them than was possible in the other pits.

Every morning and night each was well dressed with a coarse brush, and left in a much more comfortable state.

His horses and ponies would have caused many owners of animals above ground to blush with shame at their superior condition and clean shining skins. They were always doing equal work with the animals of other collieries, but *suffered the least of all, and consumed the least corn.*

I have preferred to recite these facts rather than dictate a philosophical explanation of the uses of a brush and comb to the body of the horse. Those who are so pertinaciously obstinate as to deny him the influence of this luxury, I am afraid are not in a condition to explain the benefits of such an application from any experience of the adoption of similar means to themselves. However, these are considered to be measures not truly essential, and therefore, while the attempt is on the one hand to save, as these *pseudo savants* suppose, the sum of £300 per annum, they have not the philosophy to see, or the honesty to allow another to show, that four times that amount could be saved in the feeding in twelve months, and as much more in a variety of ways of which they cannot form any conception.

We shall refer to further details on this subject in a subsequent part of the work.

PART III.

GENERAL MANAGEMENT.

THE SELECTION AND PURCHASE OF HORSES.

The arduous nature of the various conditions which attend the selection and purchase of horses, is generally understood and acknowledged even by those of little experience. There is no subject upon which buyers so often feel the greatest need of assistance and advice, and, at the same time, where greater difficulty exists in rendering these profitable and acceptable. Circumstances may arise, phases previously hidden may appear, or gratuitous interference disturb the aspect of affairs, and thus begin all the troubles and vexations which too commonly supplement the efforts of those in search of a horse.

The *tricks of low and disreputable dealers* render the process at once tedious, harassing, and difficult; while the subsequent ordeal may be fairly represented as being irremediable as well as inevitable. Purchasers at fairs are greatly exposed to the practices of such rascals, who never fail to secure both animal and money in the end, and thus provide the means of constantly possessing a trap wherein unsuspecting persons easily fall.

Some years ago a hard-working honest man, well known to the writer, attended a fair in Yorkshire for the purchase of a cart-horse. He was by no means a bad judge of the physical characters required in the animal sought, and soon his eyes fell upon one in which was concentrated, to all appearance, the qualities so essential for the purposes. Price being asked, and the animal shown through various evolutions, no objection was found. Accordingly a purchase was made and the horse led away.

The new owner had not proceeded far before a stranger, to him at least, stepped up and offered a small sum for the horse, adding, "You'll not like to take him into your stable as he's 'blaundered'" (*i.e.* glandered). And thus he continued to pester the poor fellow, while others privy to the game joined at various stages on the road, and kept up the spirit which was to secure again their prize.

Upon examination the animal was found to be a most confirmed roarer—in the language of the dealers, said "to have the bellans"—and had been *drugged* in order to cause the defect to pass unobserved.

Upon another occasion a merchant purchased a very eligible-looking animal for his cart, giving rather a high sum to a person who represented himself as a well-to-do farmer in the neighbourhood. A warranty of soundness was drawn up by the vendor, signed and transferred at the same time, and a groom removed the horse to his master's stables. For days several men—of course members of the gang—lingered about the premises of the merchant, offering various small sums, declaring the animal to be affected with glanders. The merchant took no notice for some time, but at length said he was very glad he had obtained such an animal, as a friend of his wished to have him, in order to catch the dupes at fairs. This spurred up the gang, who, rather than lose their profitable horse, actually purchased him back again at a sum very little below the original price. This animal was found to be affected with a chronic discharge from one of the nostrils, which had been arrested during the purchase by a *piece of tow* pressed up the passage for the purpose.

These tricks are very commonly practised, and suffer modification in order to render the end more easy of accomplishment. A horse but slightly lame in a forefoot is "beaned."

This consists in paring thin the sole of the *opposite* forefoot near the toe, and replacing the shoe, having first put a small pebble beneath it. It has the effect of rendering the action of both fore legs nearer alike, and if properly done succeeds in causing animals to change hands frequently.

Another species of fraud consists in filing down the wearing surface of the front or incisor teeth of old horses, and graving hollows to resemble those of young teeth. This is called "bishoping," but by those who study the form and angularity of the teeth, as well as the varied changes which they undergo throughout advancing age, the trick is easily detected. Young horses are also practised upon, in order to palm them off at a higher price as being four or five years old.

Many breeders who aim at respectability are foolishly tempted to carry out this fraud, which consists in extracting the corner, and sometimes the middle incisor teeth. At best it is but a very clumsy and barbarous plan, and signally fails to produce the appearances desired. The custom is so prevalent in Ireland and other parts among dealers, that it cannot long fail to attract the attention of the Society for Prevention of Cruelty to Animals, and, we hope, meet with total abolition.

The signs of age are otherwise dealt with, in order if possible to obliterate them. The measures, however, seldom succeed before a practised eye. In animals of great age, large depressions or hollows are found above the eyes, and *horse-copers* prick through the skin and blow in air, as butchers inflate the carcass. For a time the hollows disappear, but are seen again when the air is absorbed or has escaped.

White places, such as a star, stripe, or blaze in the face, white heels or fetlocks, and patches of white hair which are found on the knees and other parts indicating previous damage to the skin, are painted or dyed with coloured solutions. This is called "gypping," and is recognised by the different shades employed and dissimilarity of colour to that of the hair over the rest of the body. Besides, it is usually found to wash off or gradually disappear with subsequent growth of hair.

Animals affected with broken wind are dosed with shot and fat, under the false belief that the former by actual weight causes the stomach to "hang away from the lungs," and the latter "lubricates the air-passages." Neither, however, succeed with the practised veterinarian. The dupes who suffer from these frauds are usually men who rely upon the so-called judgment of one representing himself as a friend, and who contrives to come upon the scene at the moment when his opinion has greatest weight. Under these circumstances, if the purchaser misses an animal which is either "broken-winded," "bishoped," "gypped," "puffed," "blaundered," or has the "bellans," he may have secured a more worthless prize in the shape of a dangerous brute that will shy at everything on the road, kick and bite, plunge and rear or run away, after the passions are relieved of the powerful drugs which have been used. Otherwise he obtains one lame in the back, called by the rogues "a kidney dropper," or another having a nervous affection and known by the term "shiverer."

These, however, by no means complete the category of defects which hang to the horse. There are others which form admirable qualities for the low horse-coper whereby to catch the unwary purchaser, but even these are sometimes met with in animals coming from other sources; and while I am desirous of letting all have the benefit of a doubt, if such there be upon the question at issue, it is, I think, too much to believe that such screws are always produced in ignorance.

Being in want of several heavy draught horses upon one occasion, I presented myself at the stables of a certain dealer and made known my wants, but did not discover my profession to him. "All right, sir," said he, "I have just your sort;" and addressing his satellite, "I say, Bill, bring out them 'ere cart 'osses in the little stable. Look there, sir," he began, as the creature was being led out of the doorway, "you never put a collar on sech a piece o' stuff in all your born days. Talk o' pullin, sir, why I never had sech a 'oss to pull. I have been a dealer off an' on for the last forty year, an' I don't know as I've had such a bit o' mettle. Put him alongside the wall, Bill! woho, now! There! look at his legs, sir! sech pints for a cart 'oss! why, he's like waxwork itself! talk about simmertery, did you ever see sech as that? I'm blessed if I ever seed sech a splendid carcass on sech strapping lims, an', lor bless you, the money's nothink. See him trot, sir? why, he moves like a pony. Now, Bill, where's your ginger? look alive, my boy; don't keep the gentleman waiting."

"Excuse me, sir," I remarked, "you will have the goodness to spare the animal the torture about to be inflicted; it affords me no gratification, it will not enhance him one atom in my estimation, and let him return to the stall, as his qualities are not suitable for my purpose."

Rather crestfallen, the dealer said, "All right, sir, I'm sorry, but we'll show another."

A second and a third were brought out, and successively rejected, when the dealer remarked, "You seem rayther queer to please, sir." "Not at all, I assure you," was my reply. "Then why can't you take these 'osses?" and he was about to go off express again in canting description of their virtues and other qualifications, when I cut him short by saying, "Upon all occasions when purchasing horses, I endeavour to obtain *sound* animals, as they suit our purpose much better. I prefer them without spavins, ringbones, and other prejudicial bony deposits in the neighbourhood of important joints, as the work they are put to usually is sufficient to cause them to appear soon enough."

He flew into a wild and violent passion, and

declared I wished to take away the character of his horses, and what was more, called me a muff, and a fool, as his horses were perfectly sound, and I could not know whether they had spavins or anything else, as I had not put a hand upon them. He was, however, brought to a little, by my telling him the statement was much the worse for him if the defects were so plain that they needed no manipulation to confirm the appearances already present. He protested, however, his ignorance of anything wrong, and I advised him to take them to a respectable veterinary surgeon for examination, and show me the report. I here handed him my card, when he became perfectly silent, and got out of my sight as quickly as possible.

Later in the day several friends, at my request, called upon the dealer and inquired for animals of the kind. All that I had seen were brought out, and upon each occasion declared as before sound and immaculate.

To say there are no honest horse-dealers would be a gross calumny, but I must express my suspicion that many are so accustomed to chant the praises of sound animals—that is, sound to the best of their knowledge and belief—that one may ascribe such a mistake as just related to a *lapsus linguæ*. We must therefore look over it accordingly, and of course at the same time the animals upon which such vile praise has been bestowed.

Amongst the defects which are found to lessen the value of horses as well as their usefulness, are diseases of the eyes. An ordinary observer may regard these organs as perfectly sound, and their appearances justifying purchase, but alas! finds the animal either suffering from impaired vision, or, may be, totally blind. In such cases the ears will be observed to be carried forward, and their movements are exceedingly rapid, and the eyes staring, the central opening or pupil being wider than in health, and colour of the organ probably being blue or yellow. Other conditions are present, which however are only to be detected by those conversant with the different structures of the organs.

Chronic cough, disease of the lungs and heart, stomach, liver, &c. now and then is found to be present. Malformations, the result of accident or vicious propensity, may be detected; or the beast may be a crib-biter, or wind-sucker, washy, and a bad doer, no matter what he gets to eat. Whatever may be his qualities at work, in the stable he may be a perfect demon, or he may unite the kicker at work, with the "jibber," or one that will not draw.

Another may be as gentle and docile as a lamb in the stable, quiet in harness or under the saddle, and capable of doing the highest rate of speed with action and grace unparalleled, but the pleasure of sitting behind such a creature is marred by the fact that on reaching the stable the appetite is gone. The animal is overdone; and be careful as you will, the scene recurs after each journey, and is sometimes supplemented by irritation of the bowels, colic, &c.

Several days are passed before the animal is pronounced safe for work, or still further cause for dissatisfaction appears in a variety of ways; and no other conclusion is justifiable, than that the animal has been sold on account of these faults. He is sold again quickly if death does not prevent the opportunity.

In the multitude of conditions which render horseflesh (in a state of animation, not as chevaline *à la mode*) such a ticklish commodity, one cannot but be surprised at the few opportunities there are to avoid the disagreeable consequences. Many purchasers, relying upon their judgment alone, make fearful work. They know nothing of the nature, form, or habits of the animal they seek, and consequently become very lucrative victims. To purchase horses in a profitable manner requires much tact and judgment, and a knowledge of their structural anatomy is indispensable towards detecting blemishes of different kinds. Much practice is also required, but this alone will not do, as we have often known horse-dealers of forty and fifty years' experience quite as easily taken in as other people.

Bribery in horse-dealing.—Like horse-racing, horse-dealing practice is carried on more for the emolument derived, than for any desire always to distribute a good and serviceable breed of horses. Many patronize the turf under a mistaken idea that present systems improve our breeds of horses, but by far the majority have personal interest only to serve. Horse-dealing often assumes the latter in the blackest dye. Upon the turf, races, horses, riders, and owners are *sold*, and in the trial ground of many dealers the like also occurs.

"What do you want for that pair of carriage horses?" said a veterinary surgeon to a large dealer not long ago. "Well, look here," replied the owner; "all that will depend upon what you require as premium. I can afford to make it worth your while, only state what you wish." "Well, suppose you wanted one hundred and fifty pounds for the pair, what premium could you afford?" "Twenty pounds," said the dealer; "but if you will get your client to stand two hundred pounds, I can then give you fifty."

This statement is nearly verbatim as received from a great friend who was employed to select a pair of horses for a gentleman, who being in attendance as previously requested, was thus informed how he might have been sold if he fell among thieves.

Bribery is one of the greatest banes which waits almost upon every transaction in reference to horses. They cannot be shod, physicked, sold, nor exchanged, but a host of parasites hover round, "for wheresoever the carcass is, there will the eagles be gathered together." If there were no receivers of bribes, there would be no one found to offer them. Under the system the security of property is sacrificed, and its substance eaten out as by the canker-worm to the very core.

A dealer in horses called upon a veterinary surgeon in one of the largest towns in Yorkshire, and promised to send for examination all the horses he had for sale, providing they were *passed as sound, backed by a certificate to that effect, and the fee did not exceed five shillings.* In addition, the considerate rascal offered to dispose of any screw which the other might have on his hands.

Upon making inquiries, it turned out that an unfortunate individual who had lost all sense of honour and decency, had fallen into this great error. From intemperate habits he was not always available when required even to write a certificate without examination, and his patron was desirous of finding some one to supplant him, but in his application barely escaped being kicked out of doors.

Warranty.—By some there is entertained a great but fancied security in a warranty. Half that are given are but as waste paper. Many cases are on record which prove this: one will suffice. A warranty of soundness had been given with a horse having spavins and side-bones, and there were not wanting witnesses who would swear no such morbid conditions existed. A law case followed, but as usual, he who won, actually lost. The defendant, although guilty and convicted, was not worth the paper upon which the summons was printed, and a poor widow was doubly a loser in consequence.

Under such circumstances a warranty is of no service whatever, and even in others where there is no actual fraud existing in the transaction, the opinions of many upon the existence or non-existence of defects, and the constitution of unsoundness, being at variance, much trouble and vexation occurs. Nor is there any likelihood of help from the law to be expected in future, at least as far as can be seen at present. As science advances and receives its share of encouragement from the government and public, definite conditions relative to certain diseases may be insisted upon, but under present circumstances a warranty affords but very slender protection, and is an instrument of little power where the parties concerned are determined to be fraudulent.

Certificates of Soundness.—A very common mistake occurs with many when purchasing horses; that is, to seek a veterinary surgeon's opinion *after* the contract is completed. This does not always occur only with low-priced animals, but frequently with those of high value. They are examined and found defective, but there is no help in many cases, and the affair amounts to so much money absolutely thrown away. Purchasers who desire a professional opinion upon the soundness of horses, should *always* obtain it *before* the animal becomes their property. The proceeding is advantageous in many ways, and much trouble and petty annoyance is avoided.

In Ireland, in nearly all transactions in which horses are concerned, the purchase is effected on the result of an examination by a qualified veterinary surgeon. The principle is more in favour in England than formerly, and if properly conducted, many legal quibbles are undoubtedly avoided, as well as the loss of time, money, and reputation, and hard swearing on both sides. In practice, the proceeding also proves more profitable than even a written warranty. If the animal is sound, he is at once removed and the money paid; if the reverse, no transaction occurs.

The certificate given by the professional man proves as powerful as a warranty; because in the event of unsoundness, the dealer cannot sell his horse. In case the animal is sound, the purchaser receives an assurance to the effect, and nothing further is needed, as the whole thing hinges upon the question.

Recommending Horses.—No greater mistake, in the author's opinion, can be made by a professional or other person, than that of recommending horses. Many horse proprietors are totally ignorant of the nature, habits, capabilities, and resources of a horse, and in eager search for a desirable animal, meet with a friend who sincerely and honestly recommends one which, *were he to drive, feed, and house*, there can be no doubt would prove all that is desired. But, alas! as soon as the new purchase is made, the elated proprietor, well posted in all the good qualities of the creature, takes him to his own stable. No attention is paid to the different characters which exist in contradistinction to the one just left; and, it may be, a case of cold, influenza, or something worse, soon appears. The feeding may be different, and produce colic, and even death. If, however, he escape all these, the owner rides or drives out, in order that his good lady may give her opinion.

Afterwards a friend in the next street is appealed to, with probably fifty others, and at last a friend in the country. All are particularly knowing, or at least appear to be so. One sees a spavin, another a splint, a third thinks he is lame; a fourth thinks he hears a slight noise, as from roaring or whistling. And thus the game goes on, the owner fishing for compliments upon his judgment and selection, while none of the persons consulted are disposed to pay any, but feel, if they had been purchasers, the animal would not have been selected by them.

In order to detect the lameness or the fancied sounds so offensive to the ear, it is suggested that the animal shall be galloped. The owner tries his best, but fails; the friend who suggested the defect also mounts or takes the reins, and pell mell the animal goes again. He may not be found a roarer, but probably *he is found lame.* Then comes the tug of war. All agree to swear to the lameness; which is of course believed to occur from conditions present at or prior to purchase. Recriminations pass, the vendor is declared not to be honest, and he who recommended the animal pronounced as being actuated by selfish motives. Money is wasted in useless law squabbles, no one but the lawyer reaps profit, while vexation crowns him who wins as well as him who loses.

Precautions to be observed.—When it is desirable that a horse should be purchased, recourse should be had if possible to the farmer or breeder usually possessing the character of animal required. If this cannot be done, there are to be found dealers who know it is to their interest to give purchasers every advantage in scrutiny. When a suitable animal is found, seek the opinion of a qualified veterinary surgeon, who for a guinea will give the results of a careful examination, and if he cannot advise as to purchase or put into your hands a genuine horse, he will at least be able to save you from a worthless screw.

Remember also there are circumstances regarding the future treatment and *work* to which the animal is subjected. These should form a subject upon which your veterinary medical adviser is to be consulted afterwards. Let him advise as to these, and depend upon it another source of vexation is thus avoided. It is far better to pay for advice suited to each particular case, than to receive a course of drugs in after time, and pay dearly for a horse in hospital labouring under disease which for one-tenth part of the expenses might have been avoided most certainly.

STABLE MANAGEMENT.

The secrets of success in profitable stable management are *punctuality* and *regularity*. These contribute towards *the system* which is so particularly required. Without them, it is an utter impossibility for proper attention to be directed to all the details which call for notice, while nothing will operate as prejudicially upon the health of animals.

Stable management will receive a due share of consideration under several heads throughout the present work.

Early operations in the Stable consist in first making a general examination of each animal, particularly those which have been tied up by halters or chains in stalls.

This is useful in order to detect injuries from being cast or loss of shoes during the night, and to detect signs of disorder or illness, which if present are best reported *early*, on the principle that "a stitch in time saves nine."

A careful inspection having been made, the animals are watered and fed, and while they are consuming their food the bedding should be turned up, and stalls and other parts carefully swept out. Any time remaining may be devoted to the examination of harness, in order to secure the cleanliness of pads, &c., observe defects, and have them remedied if possible. As soon as the food is consumed, the operation of cleaning is to be carried on in good earnest, which done, harness and prepare for daily work.

In large establishments it is most profitable to employ a horsekeeper, who, having charge of the provender and stables, enters at a certain hour, say five a.m., and feeds the whole. Each driver as he arrives, then turns up the bedding, examines the harness and cleans his horse. By this plan animals are better cared for in the feeding, and much waste is avoided.

The duties of the horsekeeper are, during the day, to see that the stables are cleaned thoroughly, receive all horses coming to *bait*, and see to the feeding of the whole at night.

Each horse as he comes from work is carefully examined by him, also the harness, and if nothing calls for other treatment, the animal is led to his stall, watered and fed, dressed down by the driver, bedded and left for the night. The horsekeeper has also to see to their being safely tied up, all gaslights turned securely off, and report any irregularities, lameness, disease, &c., which he may observe.

In hunting and racing stables modifications exist, and, to the credit of those at head quarters, we are able to establish the principles by which punctuality and regularity may be caused to work so much good. Many ailments of the farm or cart horse are unknown in hunting or racing stables. And why? Simply from the fact that animals there are fed, worked, or exercised with the clock. If these principles pervaded the minds of those who keep and work, or drive carriage, cart, and cab horses, there would be less of those serious consequences which so often arise and mar the prospects. A young man in the racing or hunting stable, goes through a kind of apprenticeship, by which he becomes *au fait* at his duties, and habits of regularity are enforced. If coachmen and grooms in general had such training always, we should find that stable management in our towns and villages would be a question upon which there would be but little to condemn. In no other horse establishments is there such wanton waste and carelessness, or where the results are more inconvenient and harassing.

In hunting and racing stables the morning hour is from five to six o'clock. The horses are to be fed and watered, bedding turned up, and stables swept. Those animals going to work are next thoroughly dressed, and afterwards receive a small feed of corn if their work is likely to be hard and time will permit. Others merely going for exercise are wiped over and taken out for the prescribed time, and on their return receive a little hay, are clothed, have their feet examined and washed, and by this time is the hour for breakfast.

The grooms on their return to the stable dress

over their horses thoroughly, clothe, put the stable neat after sweeping out all manure, throw down a light clean layer of straw, rack up, and leave for outside duties. At noon, corn, hay, and water are given to resting horses, and the stable again locked up. Other animals coming from work are fed and dressed on arrival.

At four o'clock it is the custom in some stables to feed again with corn; the plan in the main is very good. At seven or eight o'clock each horse has his clothing removed, is carefully wiped down, and reclothed. Clean or dry straw is thrown down for bedding, the stable utensils carefully put away, and water, corn, and hay supplied. Collar chains, head collars, and halters should be carefully examined, in order to test their security for horses tied up with them.

See that in loose boxes there are no gas brackets at which the horse can get. It has been known that playful animals have turned on the gas and caused their own death from its inhalation during the night. Boys should be cautioned against leaving pails in stalls or boxes, unless specially ordered and required.

Among cart horses, cab horses, &c., which remain an uncertain length of time from the stable, *the nose-bag* is of great service. It has, however, defects, one of the most important being detrimental to respiration. The material of which it is usually made is strong and of too close texture; a coarser and pervious material would be an advantage, and avoid the necessity of breathing over and over again the same air, by admitting a current through the meshes.

Watering.—Much variety of opinion exists in reference to the quantity of water which should be allowed the horse. This must depend upon circumstances. To define a special rule for all animals would be as absurd as its carrying out would be impossible. Animals sometimes drink ravenously, and the cause will be found to arise from the stupidity of grooms in not allowing sufficient at proper intervals. In Switzerland, horses are allowed water in a separate tank, in their stalls, usually supplied from a running stream, and the results are said to be useful.

The writer has given the plan a fair trial years ago, and has found that where a given quantity is regularly placed before a horse, if no morbid thirst be present, the actual daily quantity consumed is much less. But when stated intervals are not observed, or irregularity in watering occurs, the quantity is often enormously increased.

It is from this circumstance that inconvenience and even danger arises, particularly when the animal is allowed to satiate his thirst before severe work, when over-heated, or the stomach is previously overloaded with food, particularly when water is very cold.

The practice of depriving hunters of water before going to cover is objectionable. If the rules of feeding and watering are observed with due regard to time, excessive thirst will not usually occur.

Harness horses and hacks used on long journeys are greatly relieved by small quantities of water in which oatmeal or barley meal is suspended, given when rest is allowed; about two quarts of water with a handful of the latter being sufficient.

Horses at rest should be watered at least three or four times daily.

The practice of putting nitre or other saline materials in the water, is not to be carried on indiscriminately. The advice of a veterinary surgeon should guide upon that question.

The purity of water is a question which should always be established where animals are to be kept, and particularly where new sources are opened out. There is frequently greater reason to attribute disease amongst stock, and even human beings, to the water with which they are supplied, than is generally known.

In sinking wells never select any place near to drains or ditches, privies, and manure heaps; avoid also gardens or fields. The danger which occurs is traced to the entrance by percolation of the compounds which are formed as the result of putrefaction of manure and animal and vegetable matter in general. Not long ago a whole family was continually suffering from attacks of fever, which, as usual, was for some time attributed to the atmosphere. Subsequently it struck the owner that the water might be at fault, and accordingly sent some to an eminent chemist, Dr. Penny, of Glasgow. Upon examination, that gentleman detected a great proportion of substances, the result of putrefactive changes in animal matter, which were proved to have been conveyed by the manure to flower beds in the garden upon the sides of the well from which the water had been used.

Such water has a brackish or saltish taste, and is sufficiently conspicuous to be easily detected and lead to its being avoided.

Water may also contain mineral poisons. These, however, occasion serious symptoms of disturbance, for which a veterinary surgeon will be needed to give the necessary instructions at the time.

Cleanliness.—Too much cannot be written or urged upon this point. Many disorders and ailments can be traced to a neglect of it. Holes and corners which cannot be got at regularly should not be permitted in a stable.

It must be borne in mind that the food, dung, urine, straw, &c., used in stables are all capable of generating unwholesome gases, by their proneness to putrefaction when lying about.

These materially interfere with the circulation of pure air, and in consequence the health of horses and men suffers. In order to have them removed, the bedding should always be taken from the stall, and in fine weather spread outside if possible. The dirty portions are to be separated, the whole of the floor and drains thoroughly swept out, and every portion of refuse carefully removed to a manure heap at a distance from the stable.

Mangers should always be well cleansed—especially wooden ones—after the use of mashes or soft food of any kind. Woodwork of all kinds, and even harness and clothing, require cleansing after the existence of contagious skin or other diseases. For this purpose a solution of black or pearl ashes may be used, the strength however being varied for the several purposes.

For harness, clothing, and *painted* woodwork, two or three ounces to a pail of hot water will be sufficient. But to *bare* woodwork the strength may be quadrupled.

Besides this it is sometimes necessary to use *disinfectants* of a special character.

For the floors, crude carbolic acid in solution may be sprinkled over the surface, and the whole afterwards well scrubbed with hot water having black ashes in solution.

A solution of crude carbolic acid is also eminently serviceable for the mangers when contagion is feared. The proportions are about one pound to a gallon of water in which soft soap has been dissolved, with the use of large quantities of pure water afterwards. A grand agent in the purification of the atmosphere of stables is M'Dougall's disinfecting powder, which should be thinly spread over the stall floors and other parts wherever dung or urine has been deposited.

The prices to be paid for these articles are, for black ashes about 2½d. per lb.; M'Dougall's disinfecting powder, 10s. per cwt.; and crude carbolic acid, 2s. 6d. per gallon.

When contagious diseases are known to arise in a stable, remove the diseased animal at once. Carry with him all harness, clothing, stable utensils, &c., which have been used for his purposes; do not use anything belonging to him for another; and those in attendance upon him should not go into the stable where healthy animals are confined.

Lastly, carry out all injunctions which may be given by the veterinary surgeon in attendance. He has many strong reasons for enforcing regulations which may not be understood by others. Upon these his success depends. Grooms should therefore strictly act in concert with him, and faithfully carry out his desires.

Lighting of Stables.—One of the greatest causes of a want of cleanliness is the absence of light in stables. It also gives rise to other inconveniences.

When stables are badly lighted, or have no windows, dirt accumulates, foul gases are formed, and the animal's health suffers in consequence. In dark stables the men cannot see to clean the floors properly, the air becomes impure, and ventilation interfered with. During the night, when the doors are closed, the animals are nearly stifled, they become too hot and easily take cold. They also suffer from diseases of the eyes and lungs, and in the end not uncommonly die, or require to be destroyed on account of glanders. In the morning, when the doors are opened for carrying on the operations of the stable, the air is penetrating and suffocating, and while these go on, draughts of cold air in winter produce baneful effects.

Wherever such stables exist they should be altered, large windows and ventilators put in to admit nature's great purifiers, *light* and *air;* they are relics of a barbarous age, and ought to be razed to the ground in numerous instances.

Ventilation of Stables.—Upon this question also there is every conceivable and contrary opinion. It is a subject which urgently calls for scientific memoranda, in order to apply the principles directly and practically.

An acquaintance with the laws of gaseous diffusion, draught, heat and cold, &c., at once shows that one principle of ventilation will not admit of being applied to all buildings. This is particularly the case with stables in large towns. The close proximity of other buildings, together with their irregularity of form and arrangement, greatly interfere with plans. It is therefore a matter of concern, and one not to be hastily or inefficiently adopted.

Buildings closely surrounded by others or

lying at low levels, those also having hay lofts, *always* call for a more extended arrangement than isolated ones. In the latter also there is great danger to be feared from reverse currents when the wind sets in any particular quarter.

The object of ventilation is to afford a plentiful supply of pure air to every animal in the building, to maintain an *uniform* temperature, and prevent the occurrence of cold draughts, or currents. To effect these, various plans are carried out :—

1st. Holes are made in the wall over each horse's head, opening to the outside, being about the size of a brick. These are either occupied by wood or cast iron frames and gratings, or are faced with wire gauze or perforated zinc.

2nd. Holes are also made opposite, but near the ground, and similarly protected.

3rd. Louvre boards are placed in windows at the side, or in raised portions of the roof, which also act as a skylight.

4th. Swing windows and skylights are also used to open at pleasure.

5th. Ridge tiles are raised at intervals, so that a space is formed under each, communicating with the external as well as internal air.

6th. Hollow stones or pillars are in some cases placed in the outer walls, having an opening to the external air at the bottom on the *outside*, and another at the top on the *inside*.

7th. Shafts or tubes of wood or zinc, &c., are used to discharge the foul air from the roof.

However good these may appear in theory, it is found that in some buildings the greatest difficulty exists in procuring ventilation. Let the arrangement and device be what it will, we shall find that sometimes the air will refuse to come in or go out through these scientific labyrinths, and at others it ruthlessly traverses them in fitful gusts, and deeply offends by going in an *opposite* direction to that intended.

The atmosphere is as insensible to human orders, as the sea was to Canute and his flatterers. Any number of shafts may be placed in a building, and all the arrangements named carried out, but mortification will come at the end. And not only mortification from an inability to carry out practically details which are taught in theory, but feeling of a more intense character, it may be as disease continues to devastate the stock or prolong the weakness arising from it.

The writer has succeeded in efficiently ventilating stables in the following manner. Where disease and mortality had extensively occurred previously, it is gratifying to state immense improvement took place. Coughs and colds, diseases of the organs of vision and respiration, were reduced to a minimum by the plan.

In stables where ventilation is effected by hollow bricks, &c., over the animal's head, where shafts are carried through a hayloft to the roof, and other appliances exist, *cold currents* are apt to go in the opposite direction, and thus produce not only defects in ventilation, but serious disease in the animals.

The small amount of pure air thus obtained, frequently proves as injurious in another way as the foul air within, thus establishing the dogma of the couplet—

> " If cold winds reach you through a hole,
> Go make your will, and mind your soul."

The plan, then, which has succeeded, was to arrest the back current and ensure a constant discharge in one direction only, while a fresh supply is received in an opposite part of the building.

Where ventilating bricks occur, a piece of thin leather was nailed to the top of the frame, *on the outside*, so as to form a kind of valve, the lower end hanging loose and floating. In long ventilating shafts which were formerly open at the bottom, a short tube of three-fourths size is made, about a foot long, the top being closed, and the sides perforated by holes bored with an inch and half centre-bit.

The holes are protected on the *outside* by means of a flap of thin leather nailed at the top edge to form a hinge, and the whole is then fitted inside the original shaft, but in such a manner as to be moveable at will. All cold currents are prevented from entering downwards, as they immediately close the leather valves, which are very light and sensitive.

One great objection to shafts is, that when the stables have been empty some time they become cold, and refuse to convey warm air after the animal's return. To obviate this great drawback, the gas-lights should be placed beneath each shaft, the heat from which raises the tube and contained air to a higher temperature, and thus conveys away the foul air. This may be only required for the space of ten minutes, or while the attendants are doing up their horses, after which the light may be turned down low, or off altogether, and ventilation will be found to go on very well in most instances.

Where gas-lights are not to be had, the oil or paraffin lamps, &c. should be suspended beneath, which will be found to answer nearly the same purpose.

Heat or Temperature of the *Stable.*—This is of great importance to the horse proprietor. Heated stables usually indicate deficient ventilation, but the two must not be confounded.

Stable temperature, it has been stated by different writers, should not exceed 50° or 60° of Fahrenheit's thermometer.* This is purely a mistake: for how can it be, when the same instrument registers 70° in the shade, that a stable may

---

* This principle was extensively taught some time ago, and advocated by the writer on the authority of a teacher from whom it was received. He has now, however, grave reasons for questioning its accuracy.

be kept ten degrees lower, without incurring great currents sufficient to turn a windmill?

Temperature of the atmosphere inside a building will, under ordinary circumstances, be regulated by the temperature of that on the outer; and the principle involved is to preserve as much as possible an equal condition, by increasing the discharge of air rarified by respiration, &c. But in this there may be some difficulty, as under all circumstances in summer, when the heat is great and air still, that which replaces the discharged portions received from the outside must be quite as hot. To state that a stable is always to be kept at 50° or 60° is simply absurd. Such may answer very well for winter, but cannot be maintained in summer.

The temperature of a stable will materially affect all new comers. Horses that have been out at grass, should never be brought into stables where others are confined. The only safe practice is to put them first into a shed or hovel, and gradually introduce them to work and the stable at the same time. It has been truly observed, that under neglect of these precautions the animal is likely to suffer far more than by being exposed to the contrary changes.

In all cases regulate the temperature of the stable by allowing foul air to escape effectually, without establishing currents over the animals. In summer the temperature may be considerably elevated above 60°, but nevertheless the atmosphere may be rendered quite as pure as can be expected, and to reduce that temperature would be impossible.

The object of maintaining a cool state of the temperature in buildings is to promote healthy respiration, purification of the blood, and ventilation.

Grooming or Dressing.—I must here refer my readers to page 104 of Part I. for certain facts in connexion with this portion of stable management.

With regard to implements for the purpose but little need be said. They are well known to most persons. It is to their *proper* use that our remarks will apply in greatest force.

The *curry-comb* is intended for use when the coat is *clapped* to the skin and glued, as it were. by the products of perspiration. It may be used also to the dirty legs of cart-horses when dry, or to the bodies when the old coat is to be gradually removed. But grooms should be warned against using it with too much roughness, as the animal is irritated, and temper not uncommonly spoiled, while injuries are sometimes inflicted.

The *main use of the curry-comb is to clean the brush;* which, used by the right or left hand, according to circumstances, is to be plied with vigour.

The *body brush* is oval in outline and provided with a strap across the middle, through which the working hand is put. A great fault in many of these brushes consists in the bristles being too weak and too close. They thus fail to reach the skin.

The dandy, or *whalebone brush*, is a most useful agent in removing loose and rough dirt from the body and legs, mane and tail, and should deservedly find a place in more stables than it does.

The *wisp* is made of straw and also soft hay—the former is to be used for rough purposes, while the later is damped and used at a later stage.

The *rubber* consists of linen or flannel, usually the former, made up like a towel, having a loop that it may be hung up when done with. Many grooms use also two chamois skins, or wash leathers—the one for wet, the other for dry purposes.

The *mane comb* should not, in my opinion, be used to the same extent as is frequently done. The dandy brush will perform the major part of the work of the mane comb, and the hair of tail and mane suffer much less. In fact, there are stables where owners do not permit the use of a comb, and the appearance of those graceful appendages to the horse may defy all comparison.

The constant use of a comb reduces the hair too much, and proves profitable at the time when the "rag man" or "general pick up" comes round, hence its common use. If the mane or tail becomes too luxuriant under the use only of a brush, it can be thinned in a legitimate manner; but this is not frequently required.

Foot pickers are required to remove imprisoned stones or other objects from the feet after journeys, and *water brushes* for washing them.

After this enumeration of stable tools, and the groom is provided with a requisite number, the rest depends upon himself. The appearance of a horse always reflects the character of the groom; no better test need be resorted to.

A certain gentleman, well known for his superior stable management, when asked by the writer how many grooms he kept, replied, " Three helpers and one groom; that groom is myself. I look on and *have* the things done in proper order. That is the reason you are able to admire the clean and tidy state of the place and animals."

On another occasion a smart young fellow stepped up, gave the usual salutation, and said, " I hear, captain, you require a young man in your stable, I have come after the place," and went on to say a great deal about last place, character, &c. The captain having heard him out, said, " Well, my man, I do not doubt one word of what you have said; but let me see the horses you have been looking after, and I will at once inform you whether I can take you or not."

Good grooming removes dirt and the products of perspiration from the skin, which if allowed to remain obstructs natural and healthy functions and endangers health. The proof that horses are well groomed, is shown by the clean, shining skin and absence of dirt on the finger when it is passed over the hair. The operation not only removes dirt, but causes a quickened circulation of blood in the skin. This helps to remove by perspiration useless parts from the body, and gives further nutrition to the skin and hair, hence the improved appearance, better health, and consumption of a less amount of food than in other horses.

Dressing is usually carried on in successive stages.

First, the curry-comb is carefully used to all parts when the hair is matted and glued down, *the direction being in that of the hair itself.*

Second, usually the straw wisp or dandy brush to the whole of the body.*

Third, the body brush in one hand and the curry-comb held in the opposite, to remove dirt from the bristles. The brush also goes over the whole of the animal in a thorough manner.

Fourth, the damp hay-wisp also, applied with a will.

Fifth, the dandy brush to mane and tail, and

Lastly, the rubber, to use the whole of which occupies fully one hour.

The operation of dressing horses should always be set about as soon as possible after entering

* In hunting stables, this is the *first* operation. The curry-comb is not used to the skin.

the stable in the morning, excepting of course while horses are eating their provender and when required to go out to exercise.

A good daily grooming is absolutely necessary independent of that which is required after coming from work. Those animals which have not been out of the stable since exercise need only their clothing removed, dressed with the cloth rubber, and reclothed.

The operation should if possible be always conducted in an outhouse or shed for the purpose. Grooming in stables is prejudicial, and should be avoided on the score of health.

Washing the Legs.—The use of water in washing horses' legs is often very much abused. Without care nothing produces more inconvenience.

In many places the blessings of pure water have been extolled and received as a cure almost for everything, and, acting upon the belief, the converts imagine that they "cannot have too much of a good thing." Results are, however, against the supposition. The evil consequences are, cracked heels, swelled legs, grease, &c., all of which may be avoided in ninety-five cases out of a hundred.

In many stables visited by the writer, the horses when returning from work, cold, tired, and hungry, are compelled to stand some minutes while each leg, almost to the middle of the body in very dirty weather, is drenched with water from a hose. From this cause a man is almost constantly kept to dress the legs, which are unusually affected. In one establishment, from out of nearly one hundred and twenty horses, one-third had to be thrown off work in consequence of internal disease arising. Carriage horses and hacks suffer much from cracked heels, while their breed defends them frequently from grease. All this comes from the treatment to which they are subjected afterwards.

To the mere washing of horses' legs, if conducted properly, none can offer objection. In wet dirty weather, when the hair is matted with mud, no animal can rest comfortably with such an accumulation about them. If allowed to remain, the sand and grit is moved during exercise to the wrinkles of the skin about the joints and the parts are chafed, soon becoming raw, and presenting obstinate sores. By all means let the filth be removed as quickly as possible, using in summer cold, and in winter warm water. A good brush with a *small* quantity of soap will also be required.

Next press out the superfluous water and briskly rub with coarse towels kept for the purpose, and put *loosely* a bandage upon each leg as high as the parts that have been washed, which should scarcely ever be above the knees or hocks. This process will very certainly limit the number of cases of cracked heels, grease, &c., all of which occur from the amount of cooling to which these parts are exposed when wet. If any person wishes to test the truth of this statement, let him go out of doors with his head and hair fresh from beneath a stream of water. The experiment may be repeated from day to day, but like the horse's it will be found he will never become so *hard* as to be able to defy the consequences.

We frequently hear in stables the directions given to " be sure and rub the legs dry." Whoever gives such instructions, cannot be aware of the impossibility almost which they require, unless men and horses are entirely deprived of rest. The easiest and most economical method is decidedly the use of flannel or linen bandages. For cart-horses a coarse kind of material is obtained, low in price and exceedingly strong, commonly used to make wrappers for linen goods, called " pack sheet."

Bandages are usually required about four yards long and three to five inches wide. At one end the corners are turned in and stitched down, and upon the narrow part is also stitched a piece of tape doubled, so as to allow the use of the free ends for tying.

The usual plan is to take a piece of flannel or other material of the requisite length, and tear it up into ribbons of the proper width. For large cart-horses they will be required at least five yards long and five or six inches wide. By their use the legs dry rapidly through the means of *natural heat,* and in this way the groom will generally be enabled to remove them, and rub down the legs before leaving for the night.

Clothing.—The object of clothing horses is to compensate for the loss of temperature from the body which naturally takes place in cold weather. For this purpose woollen rugs are employed, which are kept on the body by means of a roller. Hoods and breast clothes are also used with additional clothing as the weather demands, but in this sometimes error occurs. Too much clothing renders the animal sensitive, by keeping up great action in the skin, while health is prejudiced thereby. In most instances, proper exercise, pure air, and *moderate* clothing will be found most conducive to health.

Bedding.—The material used for bedding horses varies according to the locality. That most generally used is the straw of wheat, selected principally on account of its brittleness, which prevents the animal getting his feet entangled and injury occurring.

Oat straw is usually considered objectionable on account of its toughness. Barley straw is too dusty, and causes great irritation of the skin.

In wheat straw there is an advantage in the fact that beds made of it are cleanly and comfortable, but on the other hand, it is expensive in towns. For this reason tan and sawdust are used extensively in some establishments.

In farm stables ferns and dried leaves of various kinds, when obtained in abundance, are employed.

Pea and bean straw is also used, and flags from the rivers are mown and dried for the purpose.

The service and economy in each of these substances vary in accordance with the condition in which they are used, as well as supply. That none, however, are equal to a straw bed few will deny. When, however, the manufacture of manure is estimated, some of these articles may be more profitable.

In some districts farmers are prevented by their covenant from selling straw from their farms, and this causes the small quantity which finds its way there to fetch still higher prices. Under such conditions some agriculturists have no objection to allow straw for manure in return, with the payment of a small sum annually, to defray the cost of transit.

It is important to allow horses good beds. They are prevented from doing damage to their limbs or skin, and besides, rest much better, and thus is preserved greatly their usefulness.

Disposal of Manure.—As already referred to, stable manure is greatly deprived of its obnoxious qualities if it is treated before removal with that useful agent, M'Dougall's disinfecting powder. This remark applies with no less force to manure after removal to the tank or proper receptacle. Its proneness to decomposition is very largely diminished. The compounds which give rise to the formation of fœtid and hurtful gases are at once seized, locked up—companionized with other agents in the powder—and the whole remains almost a passive heap.

This is profitable in more ways than one. While the stable atmosphere is rendered pure by the use of such an agent, the air on the outside of the building is prevented from receiving contaminations it would otherwise gain from decomposing manure.

The farmer also who gets it after being so treated, receives much benefit in the greater amount of serviceable matter which is furnished to his crops.

Manure heaps should be removed as far as possible from buildings, as the putrefaction which usually goes on, resulting in hurtful emanations or disagreeable smells, contaminates the air of all places where animal life exists, and renders it unfit to support it for any length of time in a healthy manner.

When tanks or places for manure are made, care is to be observed that they are not located near wells from which water is drawn for drinking. If space will not admit of this being carried out, the receptacle should be lined with bricks and cement, to prevent the fluid portions from percolating the soil, running along drains, and then finding their way to drinking water.

Clipping and Singeing.—These are to be viewed as necessary evils attendant upon the keeping of horses. There are arguments to be adduced, strong in their tendency towards truth, and bid fair to destroy the validity of the grounds on which the practices are based. There are, however, others which are equally strong in their justification and continuance.

Both these operations bring about the same result—viz., reducing the length of the coat or hairs over the whole body.

Clipping is performed by scissors and a comb, and recently by a newly-invented machine which bids fair to answer well the purpose.

Singeing consists of burning off the hair by means of a lamp charged with naphtha, spirits of wine, or, what is better, coal gas.

The merits of each operation are considered to be widely different. While by the use of the new clipping machine a horse can be deprived of his coat in a most incredibly short space of time, simple division of the hair is thought to favour exudation or evaporation of the fluid nutritive portions which occupy the interior. The advocates of singeing claim an advantage by their process in which the end of each hair tube is *sealed* up by the insoluble portion left upon the end.

Both these opinions are worthy of being remembered; but nevertheless it may be safely argued the disadvantages resulting from the operation of clipping are certainly not covered by that of singeing.

It must be evident to all who give consideration to the subject, that singeing has much greater disadvantages than even clipping under the more protracted mode by scissors and comb. We need only mention that the flame alone is sufficient to render many horses very tedious and troublesome. Some will not permit it to approach them, while others stand trembling, and a sudden fit of perspiration at once proclaims this impossible.

In singeing also, the skin is not unfrequently burned, eyes are damaged, mane and tail disfigured. And lastly, it is a dirty and tedious operation. It answers well for taking off the thin hairs which continually shoot up during the winter; but for effectually and expeditiously removing the coat, the machine, when in proper order and efficiently worked, is decidedly to be preferred.

The policy of removing the coat of horses in winter has, as already stated, been vehemently called in question. While great respect is entertained for the opinions and the writer who sent them forth to the world, we cannot admit the constant baneful effects which are said to be attached to the practice.

Lengthened experience has taught that our horses are kept in an artificial condition, and the thick rough coat endowed by nature each winter unfits them for that condition. This we gather from the fact that in all cases of cab, hack, omnibus, and job horses, also hunters, and even some cart-horses with thick long coats, where they are worked during the murky November month, without being clipped, coughs and colds are most common. Frequently serious disease befals these animals, but if they recover sufficiently to be able to have the coat removed, nothing can be more remarkable for their good. We have seen a horse, owned by a gentleman who held these operations in aversion, after being brought off a journey in a lather, stand with the wet coat, literally starving through the night, and his evening meal untouched next morning in consequence. To stand shivering in the stable is usually considered indicative of the first stage of disease; in fact, there is but a hair's breadth between them ; and we must confess it is not plain that a cold wet coat, always inevitable upon work at these seasons, which by scarcely all the rubbing a man can bestow will not dry, can be a greater luxury than a *dry* and *short* one suitable to an artificial condition supplemented by a thick warm woollen rug.

No doubt a horse soon takes cold when his coat is off and he is placed in adverse conditions. Nevertheless, a thick wet coat must be equally productive of colds, obstructed perspiration, and far more mortality; therefore it has very wisely become the practice to remove the coat of working horses.

FEEDING.

This is one of the most comprehensive subjects connected with the keeping and management of horses.

Before going into details, we must again refer the reader to Parts I. and II. for the intricacies to be understood. The dogmatism to which a writer on popular subjects is compelled to descend, forbids the indulgence of going into cause and effect. They will therefore prove a serviceable guide to those desirous of pursuing the theory of that which we now take up in description.

The provender used for horses consists of oats, beans, peas, barley, lentils, or tares, hay, straw, and bran. Besides, fashion, and a view to economy, has led the way towards introducing additional substances, as Indian corn or maize, the locust or Carob bean, linseed oil-cake, condiments or spicy foods, and with the season, grass, clover, rye-grass, tares, potatoes, turnips, and carrots, usually called *vegetable food*.

Oats form the principal article of diet for horses in almost all parts. Of these there are many varieties, the most economical being probably the potato and Scotch white oat. In contradistinction to these, the most common are the English black and the white Tartary oats;

but in all respects they are an inferior article of food. While the potato and Scotch oats are short, plump, heavy in the hand, possessing thin husks, weighing from 40 to 46 pounds per bushel, and possessing a high percentage of nutritious matter, the black and Tartary oats are long, light, and slender, their husks are thick and bearded (or tailed), the proportion of meal, and consequently the nutrition, is much less, they seldom weigh more than 36 pounds to the bushel, and prove very inadequate for working horses.

Good oats yield about 14 per cent. of nutrition. They are as a rule very digestible, and when clean, dry, sweet and sound, answer very well for all horses doing light work.

The proportion required for different animals varies in accordance with the work; but size of animal also calls for modification in the daily allowance. Horses from 15 to 16 hands in light work or exercise only, will do very well upon 8 or 10 pounds per day, which may be increased to 12 pounds under greater work. Cart-horses will require 12 to 16 or 18 pounds, and wagon-horses of large build as much as 20 to 25 pounds.

A small quantity of cut straw, or hay and bran, is advantageously given with the oats in the manger or nose-bag. Mastication is much more perfect and digestion facilitated thereby. This equally applies to all kinds of corn.

It is not necessary always to bruise oats. If

the horse is endowed with his proper masticatory powers, no human invention or appliance will supersede them. It is more natural for the horse to masticate his food than to receive it in a partially cooked or digested state.

Among *beans*, the Lincolnshire tic is the favourite for feeding horses. This variety is small, having a thin bright husk and a highly nutritious kernel; weighing heavy in the hand, and proves a very profitable feed during excessive work.

The nutritious matter of beans amounts to as much as 31 per cent., and they are very advantageously mixed with oats and chaff to the extent of one-quarter or one-half by weight of the former. The weight of beans ranges from 60 to 66 pounds per bushel.

As a separate feed they are positively injurious. Under all circumstances they should be combined with other varieties of food, and carefully withheld from idle horses. Their immediate effects are the production of constipation and disorder of the digestive organs, the end of which is frequently fatal.

In the animal body, when properly administered, beans form a very useful agent in the manufacture of flesh (muscle), hence their superiority in producing a great amount of hardihood. The weight of the body is greatly increased by their use in proper form and qualities, and the general health steadily maintained under greatest vicissitudes.

Feeding. 159

Peas contain even more nutrition than beans, which they greatly resemble in general properties. They are, however, less liable to produce disorder of the digestive organs, being much more digestible. White or Canadian peas are usually preferred, which weigh from 60 to 66 pounds per bushel in a dry state, when they prove a very substantial and economical feed given as directed for beans. The maple or brown pea is also very good feeding.

Barley usually weighs when good about 56 pounds per bushel, contains 10 per cent. of nutrition, and 68 of fatty matter. It forms a most useful agent with other kinds of food, is highly digestible, and promotes their digestibility and assimilation. For sick and convalescent animals, a small quantity of barley which has been boiled sufficiently to swell and burst each grain, and deprived of its water, proves acceptable when the digestive powers are weakened and prostrate.

Tares or *Lentils* are not so commonly used as the preceding. Their principal use appears to be for producing a summer green crop, and horse feeders with few exceptions know little of them in other respects. They weigh from 65 to 70 pounds per bushel, contain as much as 33 per cent. of nutrition, are very digestible, and prove admirable agents for increasing the amount of muscle-producing principle of a mixture of corn.

They are, however, unpalatable, being bitter; and on this account are not relished when given alone. To use them with advantage oats, peas, barley, bran, and chaff should be given with them, which forms a most nutritious and easily assimilable mass for hard-working animals.

Hay and *straw* with bran, are articles used entirely for the purpose of giving bulk to the forms of food which occur in grain, &c., and also on account of their mechanical action on the coats of the digestive organs. By their use the food is more perfectly masticated and digested, and healthy action maintained with greater persistence and regularity.

Hay very frequently proves no better or more economical than oat straw; much depends upon the mode in which it is gathered. If allowed to stand until the seeds are ripe, greater part is shed upon the ground; and as they then contain all the nutrition, that which remains is not worth the money usually paid for it. Nutrition exists in good upland hay to the extent of 12 or 13 per cent., but in other varieties not more than 6 or 8 per cent. is to be found.

The quantity allowed to each horse is from 12 to 24 pounds. Greater economy is to be maintained by cutting up the hay and mixing with it one-fourth or one-half cut oat straw. When given in the long or uncut state, much waste occurs by the animal drawing it beneath the feet and trampling upon it. In the cut state it is very closely consumed.

Straw forms an indispensable article of diet,

particularly among cart-horses and those used in cabs, omnibuses, &c. Oat straw is always to be preferred, which in times when hay is very dear or scarce, may very properly take its place. It is possessed of nutrition to the extent of 6 per cent., but this principle is not looked at primarily. Straw should always be given cut into chaff. The practice of giving unthrashed straw to working horses is a most uncertain method, and greatly prejudicial to their working qualities. The quantity of grain they receive is doubtful, and no method can be more destructive to the owner's interest when work is required. In farm stables a great amount of inconvenience takes place from the practice; it forms one of the causes of disease in the category, which is a lengthened one.

Bran contains as much nutrition as barley. It is, however, very indigestible, and in consequence furnishes none of its beneficial ingredients to the system. Bran finds favour as a laxative. For this purpose it is given with other kinds of food in order to correct any tendency towards constipation or accumulation within the intestines. Bran contains much siliceous or sandy matter, and to this is due the mechanical irritation which proves so very useful when given with the food daily. The quantity used is from 10 to 14 pounds per week.

Among horses doing heavy work and receiving a great quantity of hard corn, bran is a most useful article, being given as a mash once a week—

viz., Saturday evening. For this purpose two or three pounds of bran are saturated with boiling water, scarcely *half a feed* of oats is also added, together with a little linseed prepared according to details which follow. The whole is then allowed to cool, and when at the temperature of new milk given to the animal. In many well regulated town stables this forms a constant practice.

In some places the laxative qualities of bran are believed to be useful in removing calculi or stones from the intestines, and on this account it is used very extensively. Having specially investigated this subject, we do not think it improbable that the bran itself has much to do with their formation. Where it is so largely used, containing a quantity of dust also from the floor of the mill, these effects are common.

During a recent conversation in London with Mr. William Ernes, M.R.C.V.S., Dockhead, Bermondsey, that gentleman stated a miller of his acquaintance once fed largely upon bran. The result was constant colic and irritation from calculi. He was advised by Mr. Ernes to discontinue the bran, or give a pure variety free from dust, &c.; the consequence was that since the time, now some years ago, there have been no further cases. Buyers of bran should insist upon it being free from sweepings from the floor, &c. Bran mashes are used for animals suffering under acute fever to replace corn, which would aggravate the complaint. They produce a softened state of the excrement, and thus relieve high vascular action. Prior to the administration of *Physic* they are also judiciously administered, whereby much pain and irritation as well as loss of time is avoided—a less powerful dose being required.

Bran mashes are *not* nutritive, and therefore should not be given too frequently to animals labouring under weakening ailments. In such cases they prove positively injurious, by prolonging the disease and prostrating the powers of the animal body. After their use mangers should be well washed out with a brush and hot water having soda dissolved in it, to remove the sour smell left by the fermenting portions; otherwise any food which is given afterwards will be refused by the animal and occasion waste.

Linseed contains about 24 per cent. of nutritious matter, with upwards of 60 per cent. of fatty or heat-producing material. It is never used alone as an article of diet, but proves eminently serviceable given in a state of solution with other food.

Linseed is laxative and nourishing. While its daily administration promotes a regular state of the digestive organs, it also proves highly assimilative, and hastens the assimilation of other articles of food. Horses which receive linseed usually look fresh and bright in the skin, in consequence of the special influence it has upon the bloodvessels and secreting organs of that part.

Horse-dealers and grooms who desire to put on a fine coat rapidly, and improve the general condition of animals coming up from the pasture in a lean and poor state, are well aware of this property, and therefore use linseed. The laxative qualities are due to the presence of an oil, known as "linseed oil," obtained by expression from the seeds. As a constantly soft condition of the dung of horses is not a natural, but very prejudicial state, care must be exercised in order not to use linseed too much. By some the oil itself is used, one or two tablespoonfuls being mixed each night with the bran, chaff, and corn. Horses soon take to it, and improve visibly under its influence, but the reader must be informed that strength is not produced directly by its use; on the other hand, *fat* is laid down, and this gives the altered appearance. Indirectly, when *good food* is used at the same time, the digestion and appropriation of the nutritive portions are carried on with greater vigour, and thus the muscular system is regenerated from time to time. The form in which linseed is given to horses is that of solution, or as *tea*. It is sometimes termed "cree'd linseed." In some districts it is placed in water and boiled until the capsule of each seed bursts from imbibition, and the whole becomes a thick mucilaginous fluid. All the trouble, however, may be saved, as linseed will assume this form quite as well and as rapidly in cold water as by boiling.

The proportions are about a pound of linseed

to one gallon of water. The whole is placed in
a glazed earthenware vessel, covered over and
allowed to stand until ready, about twelve hours
being sufficient, during which it may be stirred
once or twice. Half a pint of this is given to
each horse with the evening feed.

Two vessels having covers should be used.
When one is charged the other is to be well
steeped and cleansed and again charged, in order
to come into use at the proper time. The quantity made should not last over two or three days,
as there is a great tendency towards fermentation,
by which the whole becomes very offensive, and
consequently useless.

Among horses receiving a great quantity of
hard, dry corn each day, linseed thus treated will
be found very beneficial, and promote health.

Linseed or *oil-cake*, is somewhat richer in flesh-
forming constituents than linseed, but does not
prove serviceable as a regular article of diet for
horses. The objects of its use may be clearly
defined to be for the purpose of assisting, like
linseed, in the assimilation of other kinds of food,
the production of fat, and, when broken into
small pieces, is given to young horses for the
purpose of hastening their growth and development.

Many animals refuse it altogether; but when
they do not, the quantity allowed should never
exceed a pound pér day, as it then takes the
place of more serviceable materials and adds con-

siderably to the weekly cost, without affording proper return for the outlay.

Sheep and cattle partake of it readily; but farmers make a great mistake frequently in not using it with other kinds of nutritive food at a much earlier period, by which many diseases incidental to their stock would be avoided.

Maize or Indian corn has not proved very useful as an article of diet for horses. On the contrary, great derangement and disease have been produced in many stables, principally from the presence of a great quantity of water, as well as having irritative properties.

Maize contains 11 or 12 per cent. only of nutrition, and forms a very suitable article of diet with many others for pigs, cows, oxen, sheep, &c. When used for horses the quantity should be small, mixed with an abundance of beans, peas, or lentils, to reduce their stimulative and other properties, and *always rejected if not dry and good.*

The *locust* or *carob bean*, imported from the East, forms one of the principal ingredients of condimental foods. As an article of diet it is *not* rich in nutritious or flesh-forming constituents, from 7 to 9 per cent. only being present. The chief ingredients are mucilage and sugar, upon which its fattening properties depend. Nor does it prove digestible. Like beans, peas, Indian corn, and lentils, all of which are enclosed in a strong shell which greatly resists the action of the fluids of digestion—they should *always* be *split*, that the internal portion or kernel may be acted upon, and never given alone or in large quantities. They are apt to accumulate in the intestines, where they set up disorder and remain almost unacted upon for a considerable time, until severe and intractable diarrhœa comes on, and from which death may result.

A large firm not long ago, desirous of saving money, began the wrong way, by purchasing locust beans and lentils mixed with all kinds of unknown rubbish. These were given indiscriminately to all the animals while doing the hardest work. The digestive organs failed to extract the nutritious portions, disorder fell among them, and several, after only 24 hours' illness, died, indicating all the signs of a blood poison. In former times, when little or no attention was paid to the feeding of horses, such an occurrence would have been looked upon as an epidemic, and met by bleeding and physicking the whole of the healthy animals, by which the mortality would doubtless be increased. In this case the sagacity of the gentleman who was consulted immediately caused a detection of the error, and thus put a stop to the destructive disorder.

Condiments.—Many of these compounds, all said to possess wonderful properties, are at present appearing in the market. Their principal composition appears to be oil-cake, ground locust beans, fenugreek, sulphur, common salt, &c.

Consumers of condiments are not usually aware that when they pay the high price charged for them a considerable portion goes to provide the attractive bills and woodcuts which are so extensively circulated, and also that the compound does not possess the nutritive qualities which half the money would procure in the shape of sound dry corn. They are also not aware that when animals improve their condition by the use of condiments, the change is brought about by the consumption of an increased quantity of food. Nutrition is demanded to support life. It is not contained in condiments to the extent required, and as it *must* be obtained in order to keep up life, *the only source is ordinary food.* If any one doubts the truth of this remark, let him take any one of these batches of condimental nonsense and keep a working animal upon nothing else, excepting hay or straw chaff, and he will soon have to pay for the result.

Condiments being usually sold as secret compounds, appear to inspire purchasers with a great amount of veneration. A fine wrapper and flaming placards exhibiting a monstrous animal rendered ugly and almost unrecognisable, work wonders among the unthinking portion of the community, who usually pay double for the lights so commonly dazzled before them.

The time, however, is fast approaching when the son of the agriculturist will combine philosophical studies with the consideration of the practical details of the farm. He will be conversant with practical as well as physiological chemistry. The profits of husbandry will be derived from the proper application of science, and in his own hands will be held the key to his success.

Vegetable food consists of two kinds. One, supplied in summer, is called the green crop, and consists of varieties of grass, as well as tares or vetches, sometimes called also lints, and clover. The other kind of vegetable food consists of roots or tubers, and comprises carrots, turnips, and potatoes.

Great mischief occurs among all working horses by the indiscriminate use of vegetable food. Containing much water they cause the animals to perspire very freely, they also urinate profusely, the food is hurried through the body, and being weakened thereby, they are liable to take cold easily. They are thrown out of condition, which hard corn and proper exercise only make, and the profits and peace of mind of the owner often considerably endangered thereby.

Roots should always be given very sparingly, every bit of dirt carefully washed off; and in the case of turnips and potatoes the peel or rind pared away, as this portion proves very indigestible.

Mangold-wurtzel and *Kohl Rabi* are also used occasionally, but our previous remarks apply to them also. Among sick animals, particularly when suffering from low debilitating diseases, as influenza, strangles, &c., and during convalescence, the roots prove very useful. They are cooling and laxative, and furnish to the blood those materials which disease has taken from that fluid, but they require to be given in small quantities and at regular intervals.

Grass, clover, and vetches produce greater harm than many suppose. During their use in summer violent colic, sore throats, coughs, colds, influenza, laminitis, swelled legs, &c. &c., occur most commonly among our cab, omnibus, and cart-horses. When animals are in good condition, healthy, and doing their work well, it is a great mistake to change the diet to green food. In most instances the voracity of the animal's appetite causes it to replace natural corn, and the whole of that which months have been required to produce, is spoiled and sacrificed in two or three days.

If horses are unfit for work by reason of lameness, or operations and other causes, &c., which call for rest in the summer season, the most economical method of keeping them is to allow grass or clover, &c., with oats under certain circumstances. To expect them to work upon such food is to look for an impossibility, and is entirely foreign to the horse in an artificial condition. Green food and roots contain in every hundred parts from 70 to 90 parts of water, and little over 5 per cent. of nutrition. During their consumption therefore, animals cannot be expected to gain much support, and it will be seen at once why we claim for the horse *entire rest* while subsisting upon them.

Turning to grass.—The more we become acquainted with the nature, habits, and requirements of the horse, the less favourable does the practice of turning to grass become. In addition to the inconveniences already enumerated as arising from the adoption of green food, there are others which prove more embarrassing and destructive to profits. The changes of temperature, that of the outer air being much cooler than the air of the stable, are sufficient after sudden exposure to work great and mischievous results. In addition to the comparatively innutritious nature of grass, as set against dry food, the animal is less able to withstand the cold air of nights, of rains, and winds. He therefore suffers more or less, and not uncommonly comes up a "rank roarer." If greater fortune has been upon his side, the bulky nature of the food may probably let him off with "broken wind." Besides, he has accidents to encounter from mischievous boys, a malicious companion, or a furious bull, an opposing fence or hidden ditch. At one time he stands shivering with his tail to the wind and pelting rain, or is exposed to the rays of a scorching sun, tormented and harassed by stinging flies, from which he finds no escape till nightfall. When he should be quietly lying down to rest, and to allow of proper digestion going on, he has not filled his stomach, and is therefore compelled by the pangs of hunger to roam about in order to obtain his food.

Besides doing damage to the pasture and to his hoofs, which a hundred sheep or cattle would scarcely effect, he has sustained irreparable blemishes from which his value is considerably diminished. Taking these and many other results into consideration, it naturally occurs that there is seldom any gain in giving a horse a run at grass after being worked for months on hard corn and accustomed to the heated atmosphere of the stable, to which in a measure he is now acclimatized. When he deserves or requires cessation from work, *rest*, absolute rest, is the object sought. It may be the lungs require exemption from accelerated respiration in consequence of their tone and powers being deficient by reason of disease. The legs also demand that they be relieved of strain and all possible pressure in consequence of tendons suffering from laceration, joints from acute pain and inflammation, and muscles from damage done to their substance from various causes.

Such being the case, and probably in addition the system suffering from the effects of weakening medicines, blisters, and even the firing iron, one cannot but pause on the folly and injustice inflicted when we turn out that most useful animal and subject him to the very opposite treatment which his case and value demands. If the reader should possess an old animal whose services are no longer required, and upon their account or pleasurable associations it is desirable that he should be allowed to spend his days in freedom, after the usual preparation there can be no direct harm in his doing so. In a short time he will become as comfortable and satisfied with the cool air of heaven as he previously was with that of the stable. Nature will soon provide a coat suitable for all weathers, and in his paddock, with only a bare shed, visit him when you will, he comes with a freshness and grace which contrasts strangely with the states we have been considering. He has taken a fresh lease of life, and appears all youth and buoyancy. The poor stiff and decrepit favourite now gambols like a foal, and has thrown aside the accumulations of age, and in such a condition, which resembles the natural one most closely, he may live for years.

With the working horse matters are different. The changes are too severe upon his constitution. He no sooner has become inured to the change of climate and other vicissitudes, than he is called upon to make another sacrifice of his constitution, and subject himself again to the oppressive atmosphere of his town stable.

In all fairness such an animal should not be turned loose upon pasture land. A large loose box and yard is best, in which for the sake of his health, present and future, his feet and legs, lungs and digestive organs, he can exercise himself proportionately with the food he gets, rest and be thankful, preserved from cold winds, rain, or the burning sun. Here his green food is to be brought along with water and a feed of corn in most instances, and with a *dry bed* beneath him, a few weeks may be spent. He thus requires less time to be got again into condition, maintains it better afterwards, and gives greater satisfaction in the end.

With some proprietors, turning a horse to grass is tantamount to avoiding expense under a false belief in the efficacy of the plan. Horses that are lame or ill and recovering slowly, are usually trotted off, along with others not required for a week or two, to the pasture. Such men can have no idea what harm they bring upon themselves; they can have no idea what condition is, and the cost required to establish it in the horse's body, or they would not so lightly sacrifice it. Under such treatment we no longer feel surprised at the cases of swelled legs, grease, cracked heels, canker, inflammation of the lungs, pleurisy, fatal colic, surfeit, &c., which crowd the stables with victims under some kinds of management. Our experience too plainly shows the truth of all this, and we feel we should be unfaithful to our trust if silence was maintained upon the point. It is mistaken economy. Such management—it scarcely deserves the name—is always productive of more loss and inconvenience than profit, as is demonstrable too frequently in very plain and unmistakeable ways.

Regularity in Feeding.—In all horse establishments the system of feeding, to be successful, should be regulated by definite rules having special reference to the kind and quantity of work to be performed.

The hours also of feeding should be strictly adhered to. The latter is highly necessary on account of the small size of the horse's stomach and rapidity of digestion. Upon this account horses should not as a rule be fed fewer than four times a day. With hunters and other horses when out during unexpected times, this cannot always be accomplished; but with town, farm, cab, and omnibus horses, it may be greatly overcome by the use of the nose-bag.

When work is light and calls for little exertion of muscular power, horses may be fed economically upon oats, with Indian corn, chaff, and bran. Every 12 pounds of oats being mixed with 4 pounds of maize, 2 pounds of bran, and 14 or 16 pounds of hay, or hay and straw chaff. These quantities, which are allowed each day, will do for a horse of 15 or 16 hands, but larger horses will require a few pounds more.

When work begins to be excessive, it must be the care of horse-keepers and those in charge to furnish a food containing greater nutrition. For this purpose, beans, peas, and lentils may be taken, and mixed with barley in different proportions, *all being bruised separately*. Chaff and bran also will be required to give bulk to the whole.

If prices of grain fluctuate much or rise considerably, by substituting the more nutritious kinds of corn, horses may be fed for much less money. The details which furnish information on this matter will be found at pages 89 and 93, to which the reader is referred for full information.

There is scarcely any department of horse management wherein there exists greater scope for the exercise of economy as compared with present modes. Nor is there another where by the exercise of that economy a greater saving is to be made, by not only avoiding useless expenditure but also disorder, disease, and death, which now stalks with ghastly grin and fearful strides through many parts of our land.

There is one other question which is frequently neglected by horse proprietors. This is the *quality* of provender. A short time ago, we were standing in conversation with an extensive owner when a grain merchant stepped up and offered oats, beans, wheat, maize, and lentils for sale. Upon examination these articles were found to be very inferior, mixed with all kinds of dirt, and also soft as they could be. The prices were asked and given, and our opinion was requested. We remarked, "The samples were very inferior, damaged, and very wet, and certainly not fit for working horses." The owner remarked, "But we boil these, and their being wet and damaged kinds can make no difference, as boiling makes them more nutritious."

For the first time then we learned that to cook food rendered it more valuable in its strengthening properties. The operation appears to our mind as an attempt to *smuggle* into the horse's stomach such a mixture of rubbish that he would not swallow in any other condition. It is a cloak for the purpose of buying inferior corn, and in it may be looked for *all* the causes of the mischief which is known among horses to which such trash is given.

Without good food, no horse can maintain an aptitude for work. If he is deprived of it and inferior kinds are substituted, the body suffers, his organic functions give way, and he becomes a sufferer from disease. There is more damage done to studs from this cause alone than from any other, and what is most surprising, owners are not slow to believe in this "penny wise and pound foolish" system.

To arrange diet for horses is not a difficult matter, nor is it a thing impossible. Hunters and race horses execute a laborious kind of work, which differs from that of the cart, cab, or omnibus horse but very little. All require the same amount of stamina in order to execute their work.

None grudge the former their share of the very best, but for the poor hard-working dray horse, with his equally unfortunate companions in exile, the cab and cart-horse, anything will, it is thought, do for them. Nothing is more false than such an argument. As we grow older, however, and with repeated opportunities, the absurdity of the system may be shown up, and thus gradually compelled to disappear from its strongholds.

Feeding after work, when the exertion has been very severe and prolonged, is a matter requiring great care. Among hunters and racehorses nothing can be more marked than the attention paid to them when they return to the stable.

It must be apparent to all who give the subject any consideration, that after a severe run with hounds, sharp race, or the drawing of heavy loads, much wear and tear of the whole system takes place. It is not merely the muscles which move the limbs, but the muscles also which regulate circulation of the blood and digestion of the food. In a word, all are *tired* and need *rest*. When the hunter or racer arrives at his stable, so well are those in charge aware practically of this fact, that they avoid torturing the stomach by causing it to perform unnecessary labour. The mouth is washed out, the face, nostrils, and eyes carefully sponged with cold water, which refreshes the creature almost beyond estimate, and when that is done he receives a quantity of *warm oatmeal gruel* which has been prepared during the afternoon. After taking off the rough dirt, washing the legs, &c., he is left for a time. On the return of the groom, he is cleaned in right earnest and supplied with corn and hay.

What is the rule in cart-horse and other stables? In many the horse is first allowed to satiate an excessive thirst with cold water at a trough in all seasons, his feet and legs washed very roughly, and half his body wetted at the same time. He next is allowed to go to his stall, and during the time he starves with the washing he is allowed to fill his tired stomach with a large quantity of food, while a man teases him under the pretence of cleaning. Surely these animals, which are directly concerned in the building up of our colossal fortunes, are worthy of a little more consideration. If the labour in which they are daily engaged is not productive of amusement, it is certainly a source of profit without which amusement could not be afforded. We appeal therefore for a little more consideration for our four-footed friend the cart-horse and his allies, who in their spheres are equally as useful as any other animal, certainly an indispensable agent in our social economy.

Instead of cold water supplied in hurtful quantities, let us suggest *hay tea*, or a little tepid water with oat or barley meal thrown in. These would be far more agreeable to a thirsty horse, and refresh and cheer instead of paralysing the stomach. Hay tea is made by pouring boiling water upon a handful of *good* hay placed at the bottom of a pail, and covered with a cloth or sack.

After a time cold water is added to fill the pail, when it is given to the animal at the temperature of new milk.

In place of the heavy food, such as beans, peas, &c., we recommend for a tired horse a few oats or a little barley which has been steeped in hot water for a few hours. This is mixed with a handful of bran, and given on arrival in the stable after the hay tea, or meal and water. The cleaning operations over, and beds put down, the rest of the food may be given and stable closed for the night. By this method the animals are recruited and food proves useful, but in the unnatural systems so often carried out, it causes their destruction in not a few instances.

EXERCISE.

One of the greatest sources of health among horses is to be found in exercise. By that term we understand exertion or use of organs of locomotion, as the legs, &c., and other parts of the body more or less, not strictly called work. Exercise, or the use of the body, is intended to be engaged in at those times when the animal capabilities are not required for work. It is a duty which relieves from the close and monotonous confinement of the stable. Horses kept for a length of time without action suffer in a variety of ways. The circulation of blood is languid, digestion of food retarded, fluids which in health are formed in various organs of the body for the purpose of changing substances and rendering them fit for the system, are not poured out during continued rest with sufficient activity. Muscles become soft and flabby, and such an animal is thoroughly unfit for work or exertion of any kind; he is soon tired and knocked up. The skin looks dull and rough, the bowels are constipated, and he becomes a prey to disease of various kinds.

Exercise must not be confounded with actual work. The two are totally different. What work takes out of the system, exercise is intended to build up and strengthen. Exercise stimulates all the energies of the body and promotes strength and vigour. It causes all the tissues of the body to receive their support by reason of the tone given to the circulation of the blood, and digestion and appropriation of food. Work, on the other hand, goes farther than this, and lowers the body—causes it to waste or wear out. On this account therefore exercise must be a duty which promotes health by stimulating all the animal functions, but stops short of producing weariness or exhaustion. It renovates the body, and makes it ready to encounter excessive and prolonged exertion, which we call work.

Exercise should be taken regularly. All horses not intended to go to work ought to receive an amount of exercise daily. It is not necessary that the time spent should always be the same, nor is it proper that it be prolonged too far, as it then ceases to be useful and beneficial.

Hunters are usually exercised two hours, and this always immediately after the first morning feed, each animal having been *quartered* and wiped over. The night clothing is to be removed, and exercising rugs substituted.

Usually walking exercise only is taken, and in most instances is found to answer all purposes. If, however, a trot is indulged in, horses should never be hurried, or during a canter put so fast as to "blow" them, nor should the distance gone over amount to more than one-quarter that used for walking.

Many gentlemen prefer to have their animals exercised within call, and for this purpose a long covered ride is arranged. The stables of many noblemen are built in a square, the inner sides of which form a ride, the upper stories being brought over and supported on pillars. In each case sawdust, tan, or short litter is spread, which prevents slipping, and the whole being covered, exercise is taken in all kinds of weather. The arrangement avoids the necessity of going from home, and the chance of meeting with accidents which attend the leading of fresh animals along streets or roads, and actions of grooms in concert when beyond the eye of watchfulness.

Cart-horses, those used for cabs, omnibuses, spring vans, and sometimes even carriage horses, do not receive exercise as frequently as they should. Many of these animals suffer immediately when confined to the stable but even a single day. It is a common thing to find cases of weed or thick leg occurring with unerring regularity on Monday morning, not unfrequently also colic, and even founder or inflammation of the feet. Why should these complaints have special predilection for that day? Simply because Sunday was a day of rest. During the week each of these animals has been working hard, their bodies have been wasting, and the food taken has been appropriated to the repair of that waste. But when Sunday comes, with its cessation from all labour, the food which is taken, being of the same quality and in similar quantity as during the week, cannot be appropriated. The same waste of system is not going on. The food is not required. It is, however, taken into the stomach, and afterwards goes to the blood, which becomes overcharged with nutritious material, and as there is not time to get rid of it by natural outlets the constant occurrence by unnatural means is inevitable, those means being a diseased state.

Such horses, although coming to the stable tired at the week end, would be certainly *benefited by a walk of three or four miles on Sunday morning*. The time occupied would admit of the stables being thoroughly cleaned, the animals would obtain fresh air instead of breathing noisome odours during the operation, and in many cases ward off the attacks mentioned, particularly if the precautions referred to under "mashes" were carried out, as directed at pages 161 and 164.

When horses come up from grass, straw-yards, or rest on green food, &c., the amount of exercise at commencement should be very limited, and gradually increased until the full amount is taken. Our further remarks in connexion with exercise will lead us to a consideration of what is understood by

CONDITION.

The object of exercise is the preservation and maintenance of that healthy state or general capacity for work which is known in stable technics as condition. To acquire it, good food, pure water, well ventilated buildings, scrupulous care and regularity in all stable routine, and exercise in the *open air*, are indispensable.

Early morning is usually chosen among racing and hunting grooms, in order to avoid the heat of day, rabble of boys, or annoyance from any other quarter. Sometimes the exercise is apportioned, one part to the morning another to the afternoon. This is done frequently in winter when hunting is stopped by hard frosts, the stable yard being well covered with short litter. It also admits of other work being carried out, which would not be done if all the exercise were taken in the morning.

The usual process of getting a horse into condition, consists in the use of certain doses of physic. Some grooms go so far as to assert, "No horse can be got into condition without physic." Not long ago a certain gentleman lent his name to the statement that the Turkish bath was the only means whereby condition could be obtained. Practical experience, however, combined with philosophical examination, has proved the fallacy of such reasoning.

Some time ago the writer was thrown into conversation with a gentleman holding these tenets with extreme force. No argument could shake the view he held of the necessity for two or three doses of physic. "It had always been the practice, and would always remain so," he contended. It happened that an old vicious animal belonged to the stud, to which no man dare give a ball, nor could he be induced to take any medicament in his food, and the circumstance rushing to the mind, prompted the following queries in a way which looked at first like yielding up the point and turning the conversation.

"By-the-by, how many horses have you?"

"The old number, eight."

"Oh! is the old gray alive yet?"

"Alive! of course—when will he die? He's too tough, I assure you."

"How long have you hunted the old fellow? —if I remember rightly, some years."

"Yes, nine this season. He has carried me without a stumble, and cost me not a fraction for illness. I am never carried so well as when upon old Sergeant's back. No matter what country, he goes pell-mell, and I am sure to be in first."

"You say he never cost you a fraction through illness; do you mean me to infer that he has never been ill?"

"Quite so."

"But if he were ill, physic would be of no use to him; he refuses to be balled if I remember rightly."

"Why, the old un himself couldn't do it. Such a vagary he'll kick up if you only hold out a ball to him. Oh! he's a cunning old dog."

"Then allow me to inquire farther, if you please, How did you succeed in getting him into condition for hunting?"

The reader will understand our friend was fairly caught in his own trap, and afterwards always maintained a perfect silence in reference to the necessity of physicking a horse's inside out for the purpose of gaining condition.

The Turkish bath is also by some used under the idea that there is something always to be got rid of which militates against condition, and the poor creatures are parboiled and sweated unmercifully.

The art of getting a horse into condition lies totally apart from either of these processes. Hundreds of horses are brought forward every year without them, and on the score of what *can* be done, and *is* done every day of our lives, we appeal for our noble servant, and beg he may be spared this useless and aggravating treatment, except when illness demands it.

Condition is that state of the muscular system in which the body is strong, healthy, and capable of endurance under prolonged action. Muscle has to be built up and thoroughly developed. Every one knows the blacksmith's arm or the legs of the *danseuse* become thicker by the exercise. Their action stimulates their growth, and when after a time they are so developed, they may be said to be in perfect condition.

The muscles of the horse also admit of this gradual development. It is caused by their being regularly exercised, and drawing to them the nutrition from the blood which has first been put into that fluid from the food. Regular exercise causes the body to rid itself of all hurtful substances. Good food produces good muscle; and unless there are special circumstances to consider, nothing else is required to produce condition, excepting regularity of system.

The effect of physic is to weaken the system and retard the development of muscle and formation of good blood. They are similar to bleeding, but a little less intense. Professor Dick was wont to state in his lectures, that "physicking horses in order to get them into condition is carried on to an absurd degree, as many as three doses of physick being given to one animal prior to the season in the space of a few weeks. The first ball," remarked the Professor, "was said to stir up the humours, the second to set them moving, and the third to carry them off; and," he naïvely adds, "which it frequently did by carrying off the horse as well."

THE TURKISH BATH, AND WASHING HORSES AFTER HUNTING.

There is nothing which militates so strongly against the success of any newly-introduced measure or plan as its immediate indiscriminate adoption. Regardless of all conditions and modifications which render the application difficult, partial, or unsuited, we frequently find people rushing to embrace and hastily adopt anything new. At the same time unsuccessful use and application become evident day after day. Such occurs in almost all departments of daily life. A new toy is soon in the hands of nearly every boy in the nation, and often caused to execute very foreign and absurd purposes. In medicine a new pill or lotion, well advertised and garnished with a dazzling label, proves attractive. A simple headache or a still simpler sore is cured, hundreds rush to write their testimony on such occurrences, and swear to a great deal more, and a world wide popularity is obtained. Believers are also found who never entertain the idea of failure, and go on fully convinced if these great preparations do not cure everything, it is not the fault of the composition, and are content to live in mystery and martyrdom.

The Turkish bath and practice of washing

horses have enjoyed such popularity—they have also endured degradation at the hands of their promoters. In a few accidentally well selected cases the results of the former were astounding, but when news of men dying in wet sheets, others barely escaping, and similar results among animals came to be talked over, men looked aghast, shook their heads, and said gravely, "Ah! this will not do." As much as they had been applauded, as much have they been condemned.

In some districts the Turkish bath has been used for horses, and found to answer very well when not pushed too far.

In strict language it should be called the Roman bath, the principles of that in common use having been carried out in Rome in the first instance.

When hunters return after a severe day, tired, dirty, and hungry, the great secret of restoration is to get them clean and comfortable in the least time possible. The bath and washing with warm water enable grooms to accomplish this very readily when all hands are at the post. It is when the assistance is small that time is lost, the animal starves, and probably at once takes severe cold.

Whenever the bath or washing is had recourse to, plenty of warm water and sufficient men should always be at hand. While water is being thrown on, the dirt should be well worked out of the skin and hair. A good scraping follows immediately, and all hands "fall to" in order *to dry the animal at once.*

Experience in these matters points out that a modification of the Roman bath and washing house would be highly useful. It is not absolutely necessary that a horse should be again placed in a state of perspiration after the day's hunt. The washing may be used, but with the addition that the house in which the operation is conducted should be raised to a temperature of 100° or thereabouts, in order to assist in drying the animal's coat, which accomplished, part of the clothes are put on, and the horse is removed to his stall, when the remainder are placed. By these means, the operation is more quickly effected, there is less wear of the system than by the sweating of the bath, and animals are not so liable to take cold as the coat is rapidly dried.

The danger which is believed to occur when horses are washed after hunting and other hard work is not so great as some suppose. When all necessary precautions are taken, it may be almost said to be absent. *All that which is to be feared results from after-treatment.* Grooms sometimes ignorantly pursue a system with a small stud, few appliances, and deficient help, as if all these were absolutely present, and from such a want of forethought the greatest inconvenience arises.

Not long ago a professional friend related a circumstance which nearly cost him the sport of the season. He had engaged a groom in whom it was said was concentrated every essential of good management, having had good places and seen much experience among different kinds of horses. The groom was a staunch advocate for the washing of horses, and constantly advocated the principle under all circumstances. One evening after a hard day our friend returned, he and his horse well bespattered with dirt, but by gentle riding homewards the animal was quite dry on arrival. Notwithstanding this the groom, single handed, stripped the horse, obtained warm water, and was on the point of making a commencement, when the proprietor luckily entered and put a stop to the proceedings. Had he been allowed to go on, the chances are that with no other assistance the horse would have remained a long time wet, and consequently suffered from cold to such an extent as to lay him off work altogether.

In such cases as the one referred to, much more reliance is to be placed upon the use of a straw wisp or dandy brush, followed by the tools already named at page 143. There will certainly be no danger to be apprehended as by the adoption of a protracted washing.

It is impossible to lay down a code of rules which are to the letter suitable for all stables. What we have gone over already will be found principally applicable as *general* regulations whereby the preservation of the health and usefulness of horses may be effected, which is the end and object of all the attention paid them. The principles that are carried out in one establishment must not be taken for granted as applicable to all others. This is a too common error; and from which mischief may unexpectedly occur some time or other. With slight modifications, certain regulations of an establishment may be adopted in others with success, all these depending entirely upon the nature of duties and the influences which are extended to them. Without taking these into proper consideration inevitable confusion will be the consequence.

GENERAL ARRANGEMENT OF STABLES.

VERY little variation exists in the plan of arrangement in stables. Out of many hundreds of such buildings, as well as cowhouses, that I have visited, not more than a few attempts are made to depart from the one common principle of tying up to the wall, or manger which projects from it. The prevalence of the system surely indicates a very slow march in the way of improvement, and points out how few must be the resources where it is adopted without change.

The *tying up* of animals in numbers beneath one roof, separated by boarded partitions running at right angles to the wall, is a very defective system, and obstructive to the circulation of air in a proper manner, to say nothing of the great hardship which is inflicted upon the animal in being compelled to look at a blank wall continually when in the house.

In addition we usually find holes are either made or recommended to be placed over his head. Unfortunately, by making merely a hole we do not compel the foul air to go out there as we might be led to believe. Sometimes it may do so, when it cannot fail to rise upwards from the floor and carry with it the hurtful emanations of dung and urine. These pass beneath the very nose of the horse or cow, and are breathed to their detriment. On the other hand, we may expect cold air to find its way through, and falling upon the head, produce a chilly stratum which gives rise to sore throats and other affections. The writer is aware of such a stable producing great damage at times. One gentleman returned three horses in succession to a dealer for ophthalmia, which always appeared in a day or two after each new animal entered the building. Proper arrangement of the stalls and efficient ventilation prevented the malady again appearing. Another stable, where thirty farm horses were kept, was always productive of tedious complaints. The cause was pointed out but disregarded, and the result was total blindness of every animal.

A third stable, which is owned by a gentleman who revels in a propensity for horse dealing in addition to other professions, during the short space of two years produced more sore throats, chronic coughs, and absolute whistlers, than many meet with in the course of a lifetime.

Imperfect arrangement induces all kinds of unsystematic and unscientific principles of cleanliness and ventilation. When cold air reverses the order of currents, straw is at once stuffed into the channel and another extreme brought about. Thus one evil stalks in the train of another, and we fail to recognise them frequently until too late. But not uncommonly the results of such imperfection tell upon the pockets of strangers, and a greater hardship is perpetrated.

In order to overcome the many disadvantages which occur from the present system of tying up horses and cattle to the wall, a plan has been adopted, in several instances with success, by which neatness of arrangement and appearance are in perfect keeping with other points. The stalls are placed in one or two rows, as in the old system, according to the size of the building, which should be wider than they are usually made.

Each animal has allotted to him a space equivalent to 1500 cubic feet, in which he can breathe freely. This would require a stall 6 feet wide, 9 feet long, with height above to the extent of 14 feet, 3 feet in front of manger, and 6 feet behind the stalls. The mangers are accordingly brought 3 feet clear from the wall and placed between the stall partitions. This plan thus leaves a foot-path between the wall and manger, which is used for the purpose of feeding the animals.

Behind each stall the space allowed answers for passage in and out and proper cleaning operations, while animals enjoy a purer atmosphere, and the whole admits of a better principle of lighting and ventilation to be carried on.

The *paving of stable floors* should be of the very best kind. When holes or other irregularities are present, dung and urine accumulate in fermenting masses and interfere with the health of the inmates. One of the best materials is stone laid in large squares, or other forms, accurately jointed. Dutch tiles are very serviceable and cleanly. There are also square thick tiles used in some districts. These are made from fire-clay and burned. When laid down they present a very good and even surface. Asphalt, or coal tar, and common brick floors are used in some stables, but soon wear into holes. In carthorse stables this is a great objection, their shoes doing great damage.

Cement floors are probably the best when properly laid down. The materials are composed of what is termed by builders "hydraulic lime." The compound has the property of immediately hardening when placed in contact with water, becoming quite solid and resisting external agencies in a most remarkable manner.

Stable drains are a great nuisance in many instances. They are either too deep and narrow, or are fitted with some peculiar arrangement or apparatus which is principally designed to exhibit the resources of a cast-iron foundry. The less these things are fettered by details the better. Complications are not always understood by grooms, and in consequence such an arrangement is likely to get out of order by neglect and even tampering. We were at one time great advocates for all drains in a stable being covered, their entrance only being seen, and that guarded by a trap. Further experience, however, has convinced us that plan is not the most correct either in scientific theory or practice. Drain traps are likely to prove a greater nuisance than that which they were intended originally to set aside. On account of the drain becoming plugged up below by breaking, damage, or stoppage of solid matters, all the gases which result midway find their outlet back through the trap.

To remedy this, we now recommend all stench traps to be placed *outside* the building. The drains inside are to be made very wide and shallow, having a moderate fall to carry off the water. By this arrangement there is less danger from horses slipping, and no possibility of getting feet or shoes fast in them.

The *declivity of the stable floor* is frequently very injurious to horses' legs. For the purpose of carrying off the urine, or water during washing, the stall floor falls considerably from head to heel, as much as one inch to the foot being no uncommon estimate. This causes the animals to suffer great pain in the back tendons, and lays the foundation of lameness in that region. They are also found to stand back from the stall as far as the chain or halter will allow, and mischievous grooms strike with the first weapon they lay hold of, and are apt to cause injuries to the shoulder by the force with which the horse strikes the manger in rushing forward to avoid the blow. Sometimes he stands across the stall, and thus also irritates his attendants by ruffling the bedding. The remedy is a *level floor*. But all to whom we make the assertion at once rejoin, "How are you to drain a level stall? Look at the cost of straw when the water cannot get off; and besides, you can never keep your horse dry." The matter has been arranged by the author, in many instances with success, as follows :—

The first object is to lay down a stout permanent flooring of thick paving stones well jointed, or other hard material, perfectly level, and behind the stall an open drain ten inches wide, and about two inches deep in the centre. This is either made of strong baked fire-clay, or cut out of thick stones. To drain the stalls there are cut by means of a chisel, three or four grooves running down the stall to the cross drain behind. Each groove commences at a part a little in front of the middle, very shallow at first, but as the drain is approached they become a little wider and deeper until the outlet is upon a level with the bottom of the drain. After this arrangement has been carried out the horses are not found to stand away back, or seldom across the stall, while perfect drainage is effected.

Wooden floors are used very extensively in coal mines to save bedding, and there can be no reason why the arrangement may not be introduced to the stables of large owners of cart and other horses above ground, where scarcity of bedding occurs.

As usually put down, however, they are a great nuisance, as they confine beneath them great quantities of dung and urine, and render the stench sometimes unbearable. To overcome this, and render the wooden floors both efficient and economical, the author had several stables fitted according to plans furnished, and which were found to answer admirably.

The first part of the plan consisted in pulling up the old floor between the roof supports, and laying bare the rock beneath. By means of a pick the surface was cut away behind, in order to cause water to run backwards, a fall of five or six inches being given to it.

Next three joists were laid longitudinally from manger to heel posts—one upon each side, and a third in the middle. The end at the manger is previously thinned down in order to cause each joist to lie upon the slanting rock in such a manner that their upper surfaces are perfectly flat and level. Upon the top of these, crosswise, are nailed strong planks one and a half inch thick. At the part near the manger they are close together, but from the middle to the bottom of the stall they are kept three-eighths of an inch apart, to admit of the urine passing below.

Another feature consisted in making the whole of this to fit the stall and admit of being raised at the heel, so as to enable the groom to sweep all the accumulations from beneath. The

floor behind the stalls consisted also of a similar
arrangement, and when each part was in its place,
no drains were to be seen. Water thrown down
found its way readily and carried the filth effectually, by which the stables were rendered sweet
and wholesome, while little trouble was required
to keep them so. If the spaces between the
planks become blocked up, a piece of hoop iron,
or an old knife, is used to clear them.

Loose boxes are invaluable where horses are
kept. No stable where there are more than one
horse should be without them. They are far
preferable to stalls under most circumstances,
but are not always admissible, on account of
deficiency of room.

A loose box is a great advantage to a sick
horse. For that purpose it should be situate at
a distance from the usual stable, as a guard
against infectious or contagious diseases. It
should be well lighted and ventilated by the wall
below or door, and above by the roof, as already
described at page 140. The dimensions should be
not less than twelve feet square, with twelve feet
space in a perpendicular direction also. The
floor composed of hard impervious material,
slightly falling to the centre, so as to cause
urine, &c., to flow off by means of a very shallow
and wide open drain to the outside.

The doors should *slide* along the wall on the
outside if possible; an arrangement which is
more approved than their being hung upon

hinges. When doors are hung upon the outside, horses have been known to draw the door towards the wall by their head, and thus nearly hang themselves. To allow of fresh air, a rail or bar door is useful. It should fit the doorway from top to bottom. Half doors are objectionable.

THE CAUSES OF DISEASE, AND ITS PREVENTION.

This is a subject upon which volumes might be written. At present the information has little weight in many quarters, either from a lingering prejudice in favour of old customs, or incapability of accepting the full nature of the truths contained in the premises.

In a majority of instances disease arises from mismanagement and a want of the proper principles which insure health. Imperfect stable management is a prolific source. Much of this has already been detailed. If we need incontrovertible proof, we have but to turn to the racing, hunting, and other stables, where all is order and perfection. There disease seldom appears. If it does, in ninety-nine cases out of a hundred it is of the most intractable character, and traced to be dependent upon causes beyond control.

Among many of our farm and town studs, feeding upon inferior provender, and the use of so called "alterative" medicine, works great mischief. The common principle is to allow mismanagement to proceed for some time, and constantly drug the animals with medicines of which the groom can know but very little. The use of nitre (saltpetre) is frequently attended with baneful results. The lowering and cooling properties of this salt are such that when it is supposed that one disease is driven out, the animal is not unlikely to be affected with sore throats, coughs, and colds.

When horses are treated properly, there exists a state which we call *health*. That word means more than is usually ascribed to it, and signifies that condition which admits of *no* improvement. Of what use then are the medicines so commonly and constantly used to nauseate and interfere with the animal functions? Such things cannot be administered without producing a disturbance in the system. That disturbance is not unlike disease, and is used by the medical man to overcome, as it were, any unhealthy condition which he may be called upon to eradicate.

Into no greater mistake can owners and stablemen fall than to suppose it is consistent with reason to drug an animal in health, or that medicines given regularly prevent disease. The reverse is frequently the result. But tell such people that disease is always, or nearly always, the result of mismanagement, neglect, or want of forethought and knowledge, they would laugh in derision. "We *do* know how to manage," say they; "give us information *how to cure*." Such was the statement of an individual a short time ago. He had boasted how he managed, of his profits, and how he kept his animals in health, but nevertheless lost greater part of his stock by *mis*-management

It is far better to prevent than to cure.—The laws of the former are better understood than the laws of the latter, and should comprise greatly the foundation of every man's ordinary education. But how expensively and roundabout do many choose to go to work. Actually allow disease, the thief, to enter a stock—the stable, and even favour its entrance by taking off the bolts and bars, *i.e.*, lowering and devitalizing the constitution by medicines when the animal is in health. After the steed is stolen, lamentation occurs, and a lock—the veterinary surgeon—is sent for, and *expected* to restore that which is lost.

And what interest, we may ask, can there be in a professional man urging attendance to the correct principles of routine and effective management? Can he be convicted of selfishness? Does he sell his physic by the advice? Neither, but in execution of the trust committed to his charge, labouring under the full conviction that, after his years of study, nature is not to be trifled with, even though it be against his pecuniary interest, he knows it is his *duty* to expose the fallacy and insecurity of the support on which rests the idea that health can be maintained under such imperfect regulations and treatment. It amounts to a species of cruelty to animals, and owners and stablemen would profit much more by the study of duty and management, than that of the actions and uses of medicines which is an affair of a lifetime. Let them become perfect in stable management, it will gain them far more lasting emolument than they can hope for in a scientific path which their feet are not designed by nature to tread.

An instance of the absurdity of these daily mistakes may not be out of place. A groom recently consulted the author and desired to have medicine, naming the constituents, and stated he had been with a medical man and knew all the properties of drugs.

It transpired the animal for which the medicines were required had been dosed for months, under the supposition that she was suffering from worms. "But," said he, "it's all to no purpose, she gets no better, and I thought I would give *you* a trial." Searching inquiries were instituted, and no doubt being raised as to the proper nature of the ailment, and its entire dependence upon causes hidden from the applicant, he was sent home with instructions " to give good food at regular intervals, exercise daily for two hours when not at work, and either put a muzzle upon the animal after feeding, or allow her only tan or sawdust for bedding."

The advice was, however, thrown away. As he could not obtain medicine which was known to be not required, and even dangerous, another was applied to; the man physicked, and the mare died suddenly, her carcass blocking the entrance to the stable when the morning visit was made.

This animal was a ravenous or greedy feeder, a condition which exists as a result of some morbid state of the digestive organs, brought about originally by neglect and mismanagement. Such subjects often look rough and out of condition, and medicine aggravates the case if prescribed wantonly. The extent to which a groom should go is to carry out the advice already given, and if medicines are needed let them be prescribed by one who has studied them in a way he cannot.

SIMPLE RULES FOR SHOEING, AND MANAGEMENT OF THE FEET OF HORSES.

LAFOSSE, a celebrated French veterinarian, said, "*Pas de pied, pas de cheval,*" which British writers interpret, "No foot, no horse," and thereby indicate the amount of importance which is attached to the member, as forming an integral part of the animal body. Many have enlarged upon the theme in various ways, with not unsuccessful eloquence; others have sown broadcast a mass of error, their observations being superficial through their want of preliminary training.

To preserve the foot is to maintain the capabilities of the animal in a remarkable manner. Its anatomical structure is of the most wonderful character, and suggests the advisability of greater respect than is usually paid to that important part.

The *hoof* is a fibrous box or case, in which is accurately fitted the softer and sensitive parts. Its growth is secured from above at the coronet *downwards*, where a special arrangement exists for its formation. The sole and frog are also developed and formed by structures of counterpart shape on the inner side.

The hoof is capable of a limited amount of

elasticity, and it resists shocks in a remarkable
manner. It conducts heat badly, and on these
accounts proves highly serviceable for protection,
while its constant growth, thickness, and insen-
sibility, admirably adapts it as a substance to
which an unyielding defence, the shoe, can be
applied. In shoeing horses' feet it is a mistake
to cut, burn, and rasp them so much as is usually
done. It must be remembered that scraping or
biting our finger nails renders them sore and
useless as a defence or means of prehension.
How much more then do we render the hoof of
a horse by these reducing measures, unable to
act as a means of defence and resistance, to bear
the weight, and hold the nails by which the
shoe is attached? The better the foot, the better
must be the protection. The animal will perform
his work more readily and with greater safety,
and last the longer. Many forget the horse
has to carry weight beside that of his own body,
or compelled to draw loads and suffer concussion
on the stones at a high speed. Then why cut
away from the foot that which the animal requires so much? Some say it is to prevent the
foot growing out of shape, but that is a mistake.
There is more mischief occurring (and nothing
causes a faulty shape as soon) from the practice
of reducing the hoof, that from any other plan
adopted.

Each part of the hoof is possessed of different
properties. The outer part, the wall or crust,

grows downwards, and the ends of the fibres of which it is composed are presented to the ground. On this account it is more resisting to the wearing forces, and does not fall off in flakes or scales. The ends of these fibres, or, in other words, the *ground surface* of the wall or crust *only*, should be absolutely cut away, and that principally towards the toe, where the greatest growth usually takes place in health.

The *sole* and *frog* are capable of what is termed exfoliating, or, in other words, detaching their waste parts in flakes or scales. None but loose portions should be cut away. These parts are quite capable of their own reduction, and need *no* interference. When shoes are being fitted, do not apply them too hot, particularly to thin shelly feet. If the feet are good, and no cutting is carried on, as just directed, a hot shoe will do little harm.

Use well-drawn nails. Thick-necked nails "bind" in the holes of the shoe, and frequently press upon the sensitive structures of the foot, causing severe lameness. Besides, they act as perfect wedges to the hoof, splitting off portions to its detriment.

Let the nails be pointed with a long lead, and nail holes in shoes be coarse, *i.e.*, not too near the outer web or edge. In this there is less danger of laming horses than by the fine seam and snub pointed nail. The former nail is driven *straight down*, always having a tendency to go *away* from the sensitive structures, but the latter has to be driven *inwards*, by which it is almost certain to lame by a "prick" or "bind" as it approaches too near.

Shoes should always be made to possess a perfectly level surface for the foot to rest upon. That part of the foot which comes upon the shoe is to be the ground surface of the wall. No part of the frog or sole need touch the shoe.

The *shape of shoes* is an affair of little moment. There is no call for beauty or grand work. The secret of shoeing is to afford a protection which the hoof alone cannot give, and that is the point to study.

Bar shoes consist of the ordinary shoe, the heels being turned round to meet, and afterwards welded; or a bar is placed across in front of the heels. Their use is adopted in order to throw a portion of the bearing upon the frog, to relieve other parts which may be injured or diseased. If the frog is too small to reach the bar, punch a hole in it, and rivet a piece of leather on, to press upon the frog, and thus gain the desired bearing. Bar shoes are very useful for curing running thrushes, if the weight can be borne.

Leather soles are useful agents to protect feet which have been cut away in operations, and prevent the access of dirt. As a means of preventing concussion the writer has reason to doubt their efficacy. Shoeing as at present carried on is to be likened to breaking a man's head, and the leather sole to the plaster. It is a too common practice to pare the feet almost like paper, and then put on leather soles. If healthy feet are treated judiciously they possess a natural protection, and need no leather soles.

Stopping for feet is quite unnecessary. Grooms and smiths call loudly for stopping in order to pare the foot easily, and forget that as they pare the horn dries more rapidly, and therefore is the harder. Let them try the method already laid down, and they will find the foot is *soft* beneath the scales which fall off as soon as the shoe is removed, showing that nature uses her own stopping, which is far better than clay or cow dung. The same remarks apply to wet swabs and other allied treatment.

Horses' feet should always be kept as dry as possible when healthy. Their natural condition of usefulness as a protection consists in being hard and bulky. If disease overtakes them, poultices and fomentations are then needed, as prescribed by the veterinarian. No greater mischief occurs to horses' feet than that which arises from the effects of wet straw yards and pastures. The salts that are in the fluids found in those places reduce and dissolve the hoof, and render it unfit as a protection. Such places are best avoided unless well drained.

Foot ointments when properly made are very useful. Equal parts of Stockholm or Archangel tar and mutton suet are to be melted together,

Management of the Feet of Horses. 213

and a small portion brushed round the hoof each day. This will be found the best and cheapest preparation. Grooms, however, are often very fond of some high sounding and unintelligible name for a horse preparation, and would rather pay five shillings for mutton suet or bacon fat and the refuse of kitchens coloured with copperas, if it has only a long name such as,

"CUITOMOUTONETTAROPODOSUNGUENTON,"

or such like mummery, than be content to use a better remedy which may be obtained for one-tenth the price.

Foot ointments find their basis in the Archangel tar very properly. That agent prevents evaporation, and promotes the necessary elasticity of the hoof. Grease and fats with other admixtures are very prone to render the hoof brittle. As for curative effects being produced on the sensitive part by dressing the hoof outside, there is no evidence to show beyond what quackery swears on false premises.

Cutting, brushing, &c.—These are terms by which is understood that damage of greater or less extent is inflicted, generally at the fetlock of one leg, by the opposite foot during action.

In the former case the skin is usually cut or very much bruised, and great lameness occurs, while in the latter the hair is slightly removed from the surface by attrition, and the skin suffers in a less degree. Horses, however, may " brush" for some time, and suddenly become desperate cutters in consequence of repeated injury being done to the parts.

Cutting sometimes takes place in animals with high action, when the toes are naturally turned inwards, and the foot is carried towards the opposite leg. In this case the seat of injury is below the knee, and great lameness occurs, sometimes attended with permanent swelling of the bone, called a "splint."

The causes are generally traceable to preventible circumstances. Animals are either out of condition—weak—or they are driven too fast and worked too hard in a variety of ways. The victims are usually the horses of butchers, bakers, and other fast drivers, omnibus and cab horses especially—in fact, cart and other horses will be guilty of the practice if badly kept and harassed about. When work is prolonged too much and animals are heavily shod, they become "leg tired" in stable phraseology, and the action becomes slovenly and false.

The remedies are careful feeding and work at all times, but especially when the latter is unavoidably prolonged. In the matter of shoeing much may be done. It is the fancy to place upon the feet the most fantastic, and even the most clumsy shoes, and there are scores of smiths who may be found ready to accept a wager "to take any horse off the cut." There is no need for these, or even to mutilate the hoof, as is too commonly done. If great lameness arises, let the injured parts receive immediate attention, and keep the animal at rest. Next, place on the feet *very light* shoes, and when put to work let common humanity prevail. Horses are not machines or steam-engines, that they can go incessantly; if their periods of labour are not properly regulated, and the amount be too exacting, the animal constitution must give way. To those who are willing to recognise early signs of degeneracy, we beg to name cutting and brushing; if they are not attended to, further aggravation is succeeded by serious complications, as broken knees, fractures, &c., to the animal, besides others of an extraneous character.

Groggy feet, or those understood to be affected with disease of the coffin joint, require special treatment, in order to limit as much as possible the suffering of the animal. There is little of service to be done in a medical point of view except by dividing the nerves going to the part, thus to cut off sensory communication. After such operations great care is required in driving the nails, for if the sensitive parts are wounded, no evidence of pain being felt, inflammation and suppuration follow, and in some cases sloughing of the entire hoof. The smith should always be informed when he has such feet to deal with.

Groggy feet do not require shoes of great weight: They should be rounded off or turned up at the toe to diminish leverage in the first act of progression. In the variety of horse most subject to this disease, five nails, or even fewer, may be sufficient to hold on the shoe, as the foot is always very firm, and the animal cannot endure severe exertion. A light hammer should be used, and the blows sharp and in rapid succession, to avoid shaking, which always occurs with heavy tools used without caution.

The feet are to be prepared according to rules already given at page 210.

Sidebones among cart-horses are very common. When the natural elasticity of the cartilages which surmount the wings of the coffin bone is lost, the parts are found to have been involved in the process of inflammation and subsequent conversion into bone (ossification.) The motion of the joint is more or less interfered with, concussion causes pain, and the tendency is towards an increase of size.

If the feet are properly preserved and prepared for the shoe, all that is required is to keep the heels and toes low and stiff, and beneath the sidebone; the heel of the shoe is best made to pass *straight backwards from the quarter*, in order to extend the surface of bearing. The foot should be hammered as lightly as possible.

For *ring bones* the toes and heels of shoes should also be kept low, in order to avoid concussion

In all cases, however, where these affections are of long standing, and medical treatment produces little or no good, lameness being persistent, the animal will be of scarcely any service for town work. It is best to place them upon soft land in the farmer's hands, where many kinds of light work may be performed without any sacrifice of feeling or increase of suffering to the animal.

Under certain aggravated conditions of the three forms of disease we have been considering, the advice of a veterinary surgeon should be sought as to the policy of such animals being retained whose life can only be one of protracted misery.

Pumiced feet, so called, are of frequent occurrence among cart-horses, but others also are liable when mismanagement occurs. The appearances which give rise to the term are convexity of the sole and concavity of the wall, with great tendency to elongation towards the toe. They are the outward manifestations of an inward diseased state of the sensitive and secreting structures—hence the deformed shape and growth.

Shoeing may greatly palliate the case, but nothing is known that will cure it. Put on a strong shoe having a great amount of cover to protect the sole. Seat or hollow out the upper surface, that no part but the wall shall receive weight. Let the heels and toe be low and stiff; keep the toe of the hoof moderately short; avoid paring the sole, or otherwise reducing the foot; use well-drawn nails, put well up; keep on the shoe always as long as it is secure and serviceable, so as to avoid breaking the foot by too frequent removes. Use daily dressings of hoof ointment, inside and out, after the foot is cleaned, by which means many animals will be enabled to perform a great amount of work with ease and cheerfulness.

Pricks and binds are the natural consequences of the system of shoeing with nails. Some persons ignorantly suppose they can only occur from carelessness. They must, however, be informed that workmen of the best class, well known for their superior skill and care, are liable to cause lameness by a prick or bind with the nail in shoeing. There are many causes for it, most of which are beyond his control. Great mischief ensues frequently after such an occurrence, and the difficulty commences in attaching the blame to the proper person. In ninety-nine cases out of a hundred such ought not to occur, yet it does, and how? As soon as a horse is lame he is usually walked off to the smith, who receives the information that he has pricked the horse. Knowing the estimate placed by owners generally upon such a case, the smith naturally endeavours to prove the contrary, and in many cases succeeds by ignorance of the proper symptoms and mode of manipulation, in having the horse sent home with the qualifying announcement, that the lameness is in the shoulder or other place, " but not in the foot."

At this stage, simple matters would set the

animal sound in a few hours, but alas! too frequently delay occurs, or some quack treatment is pursued, and at length matter issues from the coronet, and the foot is diseased and disfigured for life.

In all cases of lameness, the shoe should be removed, and foot properly examined by percussion with the hammer, and pressure by the pincers. The situation of nail holes in the hoof will determine if some are too near, and evidences of pain will usually point to the part under trial.

If the lameness is not great, mere removal of the shoe and nails will mostly be sufficient; or a warm poultice of bran or sawdust may be applied for twelve hours. If, on the other hand, the pain and lameness be excessive, having *gradually* increased in severity, matter may be suspected to be present within the hoof. Exploration with the knife should follow percussion and pressure, by which the precise spot will be detected, and exit thus given to the imprisoned pus will afford almost instant relief. Poultices preceded by hot fomentations will be required, besides other treatment, to allay febrile excitement and expedite the case, for which a qualified veterinarian is best to dictate, according to existing circumstances.

It is advisable in all cases of lameness to apply at once to a veterinary surgeon; much tediousness and disappointment as well as expense may be avoided. As in many other cases, "the first cost is the least in the end."

The shoeing of lame horses requires special measures, and could not be treated any further in a work of this kind without extending it beyond ordinary limits. The instructions already given will in greater part be found applicable. By their observance much harm may be avoided, and the usefulness of our valuable servants greatly extended. Brittle feet, so called, may be wonderfully restored in a short time, the falling off or losing of shoes greatly avoided; and remember that the greater evil exists in doing too much, rather than knowing what should *not* be done.

Horse-shoeing in coal-mines fully exemplifies this statement. Here, where the smiths have many horses and ponies to shoe after working hours in the pit have ceased, the benefits of not doing too much are to be observed. There is seldom to be seen a bad foot. Except where the roadways are saturated or overflowing with water having mineral salts in solution, such may be said scarcely to occur. Animals are also very seldom lamed in shoeing. When they run upon dry ground the feet grow thick and strong. At each shoeing the smith merely cuts down the foot to produce a level surface, "lets in the clip" to the required distance at the toe backwards, nails on the shoe, clenches and roughly rasps off overhanging portions. By these means the shoes are seldom lost, and the best of feet are found.

It is a pity the system cannot be exhumed in

greater part from the coal-mines, and transferred for the benefit of our town and other horses in parts where proper care is not exercised. Anything likely to prove beneficial, even if brought from a coal-mine, would be acceptable, and the value of our horses demands this consideration.

POULTICES AND FOMENTATIONS.

There is frequently great need of these agents as auxiliaries to the treatment of disease which arises among horses. In contradistinction to the great amount of good which they may be caused to effect, much harm may ensue by ignorance or misunderstanding.

A poultice is employed for two purposes—to apply heat and moisture conjointly to a part, or cold and moisture. We have therefore warm and cold poultices. Fomentations, on the other hand, are always hot. They consist usually of water alone, or infusions of some plant whose active principle has some medicinal effect.

The object in either case is to perpetuate in a part by external means, either a degree of heat or cold which cannot be effected otherwise, in order to promote some desirable curative action. To render these means effective, their use must be long continued, and the desired temperature maintained as near as possible. A poultice loosely applied, or a fomentation imperfectly maintained, produces absolute harm by the evaporation and cooling which ensues, and its effects upon the internal structures. When parts have been fomented or poulticed, they should either be dried or protected by covering from the atmosphere.

In the treatment of wounds or abscesses, neglect of these precautions produces serious obstructions to the successful recovery of a case, and the medical attendant too frequently incurs undeserved censure.

SENDING FOR THE VETERINARY SURGEON.

In the hurry and excitement consequent upon sudden accident or illness among animals, messengers are frequently despatched with imperfect reports, and therefrom much error and inconvenience results. These facts may be sufficient excuse for appending a few plain rules to be observed in order to avoid the occurrence of untoward events, and rather expedite matters towards a favourable if not successful issue.

First.—As far as possible always send a written message. Never trust verbal messages to boys or illiterate persons; and let the name and address be legibly inscribed.

Second.—Send *early*, that the practitioner may see the case before it is aggravated by serious and irrecoverable complications. "A stitch in time saves nine," and the first cost may avoid the necessity of incurring greater ones.

Thirdly.—Afford as much information as possible as to what has been observed of the *symptoms* manifested by the animal. The practitioner may be greatly assisted in preparation of remedies to take with him. Never send such a message as "You are to come directly, we have a horse (or cow) badly." This is a very useless and perplexing statement.

Fourthly.—Avoid absolute doctoring the animal for which you desire a professional opinion. Attend implicitly to the instructions received, and success will be more certain.

Fifthly.—Never withhold information upon matters which are calculated to throw light upon the causes, nature, symptoms, &c., of the ailment. Absence of such paralyses the hands of skill, and prevents the adoption of proper measures.

These may admit of some variation under certain circumstances, but in the majority of cases, if carried out properly, they will effect more good than is to be expected at the present day in many places, from the utter disregard of system which prevails, particularly in agricultural districts.

INDEX.

Ability, 48.
Absorption, 24.
Acids of digestion, 29.
Advantages of proper food and system, 42, 46.
,, clipping and singeing, 154.
,, loose boxes, 201.
,, sliding doors, 201.
Albumen, 30.
Albuminous principles of food, 28—30.
Albuminuria, 45.
Animal heat, 32.
,, not maintained by fat alone, 35.
,, produced in part from nitrogenous compounds, 32.
Animals hybernating, 35.
,, tying up of, 194.
Arrangement of stables, 194.
Assimilation, 24.

Bad arrangements of stables, ill effects of, 195.
Bandages, use of, 149.
Barley, 150.
Bar-shoes, 211.
Bean and pea-straw, 101.
Beans, 158.
,, require to be bruised, 175.
Bearing horses, 113.
Bedding, 150.
Bellows or roaring, 112.
Bishoping, 114.
Black-ashes as a detergent, 135.
Blaunders or glanders, 112.
Body-brush, 143.
Boussingault and Papin, experiments to determine whether horses pass grain unchanged, 60.
Bran : its nature, uses, and abuses, 83, 161.
,, mashes, 162
,, as a laxative, 84.
Breeding or pluck, 48.

Bribery in horse dealing, 120.
Broken wind, how caused, 21.
,,   how disposed of, 115.
Bruised corn, economy of, 99.
Bruising oats, not always necessary, 157.
,,   peas, beans, &c., necessity for, 175.
Brushes, 143.
Brushing, 213.
Bulk or volume, 39.

Cæcum, 25.
,,   contains fluids principally, 23.
Calculi or stones in the intestines, 51, 162.
,,   ,,   their origin, 51, 52, 162.
,,   ,,   usual composition, 52.
,,   ,,   presented by Mr. Foreman, M.R.C.V.S., 54.
Capacity of large intestines, 26.
,,   small ditto, 24.
Carbolic acid as a disinfectant, 135.
Care required in feeding after work, 60, 178.
Carob bean, 166.
Carrots and turnips, 98, 169.
Caseine, 30.
Causes of cutting and brushing, 213.
,,   disease, and its prevention, 203.
Certificates of soundness, 123.
Chaff, economy of, 99.
Changes in chyme, 27.
Change of grain, objections to, 82.
Cheap food, what constitutes a, 81.
Cheeks, 14.
Choking, causes of, 19.
Chronic cough, one of the causes of, 22.
Chyle, 24.
Chyme, 27.
,,   changes in, 27.
Cleanliness, 104, 134.
Clipping and singeing, 152.
Clothing, 150.
Coal mines, feeding in, 2, 79, 85.
,,   neglect of horses and ponies in, 77, 105.
,,   shoeing in, 220.
Colon, 25.
Colliery estates, systems of feeding adopted upon, 74, 76, 79, 85.
Condiments, 103, 167.
Condition, 185.
,,   physic not always required for, 186

Consequences of an imperfect system of feeding in coal mines, 2, 75, 76.
Cooked food, 18, 42, 101.
,, does not render food more digestible or nutritious, 41.
,, diseases arising from, 45, 101.
,, is expensive, 44.
,, injurious effects of, 18, 45, 101.
,, not economical, 55.
Corn, mixture of, 89.
Cost of feeding horses in Sheffield, 72.
,, ,, ,, upon oats, 65.
Cough, chronic, how caused, 22.
Cree'd linseed, 164.
Cubic space required by each animal, 196.
Currycomb, 143.
Cut food promotes salivation, 75.
,, ,, use of, 160.
Cutting and brushing, 213.

DANDY-brush, 144.
Danger of gas-brackets in stables, 131.
,, the indiscriminate use of drugs, 133, 206.
Dealers, tricks of, 111.
Declivity of stable floors, 198.
Defects of horses, 119.
Deglutition, 17, 19.
Development and maintenance, 8.
Diabetes, 13, 42.
Digestion, organs of, 14, 108.
,, ,, should be in a healthy condition, 60.
,, acids of, 29.
,, in stomach, 22.
,, in intestines, 27.
,, rapid in horse, 22, 56.
Digestive process, 26.
Diseases arising from cooked food, 45, 101.
,, induced by the use of impure bran, 162.
,, causes and prevention of, 203.
,, produced by badly arranged stables, 195.
Disinfectants, 135.
Disposal of manure, 151.
Do horses masticate the whole of their grain? 56, 60.
Doors, sliding, 201.
Drain or stench traps, 198.
Drains in stables, 197.
Dressing or grooming, 104, 143.
Dry food, objections to, 54

Dung or fæces, 29.
Duodenum, 24.
Dyeing, 115.

EARLY operations in the stable, 128.
Economy of food, 71, 176.
    „ of using chaff and bruised corn, 99.
Effects of badly arranged stables, 195.
Effete or useless matter, 11, 29.
Efficiency of gas lights in ventilation, 141.
Elementary principles of food, 28.
Ernes, Wm., Esq., M.R.C.V.S., his experience on the exclusive use of bran, 162.
Errors to be avoided, 40, 96.
Essential characters of food, 29.
    „ qualities of oats, 65.
    „   „ other corn, &c. 156.
Evil effects of insufficient food for young animals, 12.
Exercise, 181.
    „ importance of, for hard-working horses, 183.
Experiments of Boussingault and Papin, 60.
Extracting temporary teeth, custom of, in Ireland, 114.
Eyes, disease of, 119.

FALLACIOUS ideas as to the passage of unchanged grain, 54, 58, 60.
Fat or heat producers, 28, 32.
Feeding, 156.
    „ after work, 23, 178.
    „ economy of, 55, 74, 80, 176.
    „ manger system of, 55.
    „ regular, 23, 46, 50, 175.
    „ saving effected in, by Mr. Hunting, 74.
    „ saving effected by Mr. Scott at Hetton Colliery, 80.
    „ system of, at the Londonderry Collieries, 85.
    „   „ at the Hetton Colliery, 76.
Feet of horses, their shoeing and management, 208.
    „   „ stopping of, 212.
Fibrine, 30, 31.
Flesh formers, 28.
Floors, wooden, 199.
    „ declivity of, 198.
Fluids, passage of, 23.
Fæces or dung, 29.
Food, advantages of good, 12, 42, 46.
    „ economy of, 71, 176.
    „ elementary principles of, 28, 29.
    „ essential characters of, 29.

Index. 231

Food green, 97, 169.
,, immediate object of, 8.
,, indigestible parts of, 29.
,, insufficient, effects of, on young animals, 12.
,, relative proportions of nutritious and starchy matter in, 63.
,, requires bulk or volume, 39.
,, steamed, objectionable, 87.
,, varieties of, 63, 156.
,, when cooked expensive, innutritious, and not economical, 18, 42, 55, 101.
Foot ointments, 212.
,, pickers, 145.
Foreman, Thos., M.R.C.V.S., collects specimens of calculi, 54.
Forms of mixture of grain, 89.
Frog, the, 210.

Gas-brackets in stables, danger of, 131.
,, lights, their efficacy, in ventilation, 141.
Gastric juice, 26.
,, digestion, 26.
General arrangement of stables, 194.
Glanders or blaunders, 112.
Gluten, 30, 31.
Grain, economy in storing, 68.
,, objections to a change of, 62.
,, selection and purchase of, 68, 156.
,, does it pass unacted upon? 57, 58, 60.
Grass, turning horses to, 171.
Green food, 97, 169.
Grinders, 15.
Groggy feet, 215.
Grooming, 104, 143.
Gruel after work, 178.
Gullet, 15.
Gypping, 115.

Hard work, care required in feeding horses after, 23, 60, 173.
Hay and straw, 99, 101, 160.
,, tea after work, 179.
Health, what is it? 204.
Healthy condition of digestive organs necessary, 60.
Heat, animal, 32.
,, producers, 28, 32.
,, ,, relative proportion of, in food, 63.
,, or temperature of stable, 141.
Heavy draught horses objectionable, 49.
Hetton Colliery system of feeding, 76.

Horse, digestive organs of, not intended for cooked or sloppy food, 41.
Horse dealing, bribery in, 120.
  ,, shoeing in coal mines, 220.
Horses, defects in, 119.
  ,, recommending, 124.
  ,, feet should be dry, 212.
  ,, their selection and purchase, 111.
Hoof, the, 208.
Hours of work of pit animals, 77.
How to prevent cutting and brushing, 214.
Hunting, C., M.R.C.V.S., his determination of the proportion of husk in oats, 67.
  ,,   ,, his saving in the feeding at South Hetton, 74.
Husk in oats, proportion of, in different varieties of, 67.
Hybernating animals, 35.

IDENTITY of nitrogenous compounds from all sources, 31.
Ilium, 24.
Ill effects of maize, 70.
Importance of exercise for hard working horses, 183.
Importance of grooming, 104, 143.
  ,, of prevention, 4, 46, 203.
Impure bran, a cause of disease, 162.
Immediate objects of food, 8.
Incisor teeth, 14.
  ,, ,, practice of extracting, 114.
Indian corn, 70, 166.
Indigestible parts of food, 29.
Inflating the skin, or "puffing the glym," 114.
Insalivation, 16.
Insufficient food, evil consequences of, in young animals, 12.
Intestines, stones or calculi in, 51, 142.
  ,, their capacity and division, 26.
Injurious effects of cooked food, 18, 45, 87, 101.
  ,, ,, insufficient food in young animals, 12.
Ireland, mode of selling horses in, 124.

JEJUNUM, 24.
Jibber, the, 119.

KIDNEY-dropper, 116.
Kohl-rabi, 169.

LACTEALS, or absorbents, 24.
Lameness, foot should always be examined in, 210.

Index.

Lameness in horses, how disguised, 113.
Large intestines, 25.
Large number of horses, importance of a superintendent for, 61.
Laxative, bran as a, 84, 161, 162.
Leather soles, 211.
   ,, valves used in ventilation, 140.
Legs, washing the, 147.
Leguminous seeds require bruising, 99, 175.
Lentils, 159.
Level floors, necessity for, 199.
Lighting of stables, 136.
Linseed, 71, 163.
   ,, or oil cake, 165.
   ,, ,, value of, for young stock, 166.
   ,, oil as an improver of condition, 164.
   ,, tea, 164.
Locust or carob-bean, 166.
Londonderry Collieries, system of feeding adopted, at, 85.
Long fasts prejudicial, 23, 78.
Longevity promoted by good food, 40.
Loose boxes, 201.

McDougall's disinfecting powder, 135, 151.
Maintenance, 10.
Maize or Indian corn, 70, 166.
Management of horses' feet, 208.
Mane comb, 144.
Manger system, 55.
Mangold wurtzel, 169.
Manure, disposal of, 41.
Mashes of bran, 162.
Mastication, 15.
Materials for stable floors, 197.
Medicines, danger of their indiscriminate use, 206.
Mesenteric glands, 28.
Metamorphosis of tissue, 10, 11.
Mismanagement, 1.
Mixtures of corn or grain for horses, 89.
Moisture, injurious effects of, on horses' feet, 212.
Molar teeth or grinders, 15.
Mortality from mismanagement, 5, 7, 13.
   ,, saved by Mr. Hunting's system, 75.
   ,, ,, ,, Scott's ditto, 81.

Nails in shoeing, 210.
Nature, uses, and abuses of bran, 83, 161, 162.
Neglect of grooming pit animals, 105.

Nitrogenous compounds, their identity from all sources, 30.
„ principles of food, 30, 63, 156.
Non-nitrogenous principles of food, 32.
„ „ relative proportion of, in different kinds of food, 63, 156.
Nose-bags, 131.

OATS, 64, 156.
„ cost of feeding upon, 65.
„ do not always require bruising, 157.
„ essential qualities of, 65.
„ proportion of husk in, 67.
„ quantity to be used, 157.
„ straw, 99.
Objections to a change of grain, 83.
„ to green food, 97, 170.
„ to the use of dry food, 54.
Œsophagus, 15.
Oil-cake, 165.
„ „ value of, for young stock, 166.
Ointment for feet, 212.
Organs of digestion, 14, 108.
Origin of calculi, 52, 162.

PATENT baked food, 104.
Paving of stable floors, 196.
Pea and bean straw, 101.
Peas, 159.
„ and beans should be bruised, 175.
Pharynx, 15.
Pit animals are much neglected, 77, 105.
„ their hours of work, 77.
„ horsekeepers have too many animals under their care, 105.
Pluck or breeding, 48.
Precautions to be observed in feeding, 23, 46, 50, 96, 167, 170.
„ to be observed in purchasing horses, 126.
Prehension, 14.
Prejudice against system on colliery estates, 4, 77, 87, 108.
Prevention, importance of, 4, 46, 205.
Pricks and binds in shoeing, 218.
Process of digestion, 26.
Profuse staling, 42.
Proportion of husk in different kinds of oats, 67.
Provision for maintaining warmth in the body, 35.
Ptyalin, 16.
Puffing the glym, 114.
Pumiced feet, 217.

Purchase and selection of horses, 111.
,, ,, ,, precautions to be observed in, 126.
Purity of water, 133.
Putrefaction, its effects upon drinking water, 133.

RAPIDITY of digestion, 22.
Recommending horses, 124.
Rectum, 25.
Regular feeding, 23, 46, 50, 175.
Relative proportion of heat producers in different kinds of food, 63.
,, ,, nutritious matter in different kinds of food, 31, 63.
Ring-bones, 216.
Roaring or "bellans," 112.
Roots, 98, 169.
Rubber, the, 144.
Rules, simple, for shoeing, 208.

SACCHARINE principles of food, 17, 28, 32, 63.
Saliva, 16.
,, is secreted abundantly, 17.
,, chemical action of, 17.
,, flow of, promoted by cut and dry food, 75, 99.
,, cannot be replaced by any artificial agent, 18.
,, quantity of, an important agent in digestion, 17, 99.
,, solvent action of, 16.
,, general uses of, 17, 18.
Saving effected by Mr. C. Hunting, 74.
,, ,, by systematic feeding, 102.
,, ,, by Mr. L. Scott, 79.
Selection and purchase of grain, 68.
,, ,, horses, 111.
Sending for the veterinary surgeon, 224.
Sheffield, cost of feeding horses in, 72.
Shiverer, the, 116.
Shoe, necessity for its removal in all cases of lameness, 219.
Shoeing, pricks and binds in, 218.
Shoes, their shape, 211.
Side-bones, 216.
Singeing, 152.
Sliding-doors, 201.
Small intestines, 24.
Sole and frog, 210.
Soles, leather, 211.
Soundness, certificates of, 123.

Spicy foods or condiments, 103, 167.
Stable management, 128.
Stable, early operations in, 128.
  ,, drains, 197.
  ,, floors, materials for, 196.
  ,, declivity of, 198.
  ,, paving of, 196.
  ,, should be level, 199.
Stable-tools, 143.
  ,, ,, use of, 146.
Stables, arrangement of, 194.
  ,, lighting of, 136.
  ,, various modes of ventilating, 137.
Staling, profuse, 42.
Steamed food objectionable, 86.
Stench traps, 193.
Stomach of horse, ox, and man, 20.
  ,, small, 21.
  ,, of ox divided into four parts, 20.
Stones or calculi in intestines, 51.
  ,, ,, their origin, 52, 162.
Stopping for feet, 212.
Storing of grain, 68.
Straw as provender, 99, 101, 160.
Strength or ability derived from food, 48.
  ,, not weight, required for moving heavy loads, 49.
Superintendent, importance of a, 61.
Swallowing, 17, 19.
System of feeding in various collieries, 75, 85.
  ,, ,, saving to be effected by a complete, 102.

Tares or lentils, 71, 159.
Teeth, incisor, 14.
  ,, molar, 15.
  ,, extraction of, to accomplish fraud, 114.
Temperature of stables, 141
  ,, ,, its effects upon all new comers, 142.
Tissue, metamorphosis of, 10, 11.
Tongue, 14.
Tricks of dealers, 111.
Turkish bath, as an aid to condition, 187.
  ,, ,, the, and washing horses after hunting, 109.
Turning to grass, 171.
Turnips and carrots, 98, 169.
Tying up of animals, 194.

Undigested food, 29.
  ,, grain, passage of, 57, 58, 60.

Urination, profuse, 42.
Use of dry food, objections to the, 54.
    ,, stable tools, 146.
Useless or effete matters, 11.
Uses and abuses of bran, 83, 162.
    ,, saccharine principles of food, 17, 28, 32.
    ,, saliva, 17.

VARIETIES of food, 63.
Various forms of mixing grain, 89.
Vegetable food, 160.
Ventilation of stables, 137.
    ,, by the use of leather valves, 140.
    ,, various modes of, 138.
Veterinary surgeon, sending for the, 224.

WALL, the, 209.
Want of condition, effects of, 13, 97, 213.
Warranty, 122.
Washing horses, 189.
Washing the legs, 147.
Waste of animal tissues, 10, 11.
Wasting of the body, causes of, 34.
Water brushes, 145.
Water, purity of, 133.
Watering, 132.
What constitutes a cheap food, 81.
Wisp, the, 144.
Woolen floors, 199.
Work, feeding after, 60, 178.

YOUNG animals require good food, 12.

THE END.

www.ingramcontent.com/pod-product-compliance
Lightning Source LLC
Chambersburg PA
CBHW031731230426
43669CB00007B/315